"[*Black Men and Depression*] is a brave, unblinking look at what it is like to be an African American man with depression. John Head's insightful analysis of the connection between racism and this illness should be required reading for everyone who cares that African American men are often absent from their families, are in jails and prisons in disproportionate numbers, and die at an alarming rate from suicide." —Cynthia Wainscott, Chair, National Mental Health Association

"John Head deftly takes us on a personal and cultural journey into the nature of depression and the social stigmas that surround it. [*Black Men and Depression*] is an insightful, compelling and practical guide." —Lawrence Kutner, Ph.D., Co-Director, Harvard Medical School Center for Mental Health and Media

"One of the enduring myths about depression is that it is the province of some special group—the creative genius, maybe, or middle-class white people. John Head explodes the last myth with his frank and exhaustive look at depression among black men in America, using as a starting point the most authentic evidence possible: his own life. Neither a polemic nor a weepy tell-all, [*Black Men and Depression*] is a sobering look at what the world's most common mental illness is doing to a big chunk of our population—with well-researched words of hope and help for those men and the people who love them."—Tracy Thompson, author of *The Beast: A Reckoning with Depression*

"John Head's [*Black Men and Depression*] is a 'must read' for the black man suffering from the lingering, tormenting blues and for anyone who knows him. Head makes the experience of depression real in heartfelt, well-crafted vignettes that give substance to his demand that we acknowledge, name, understand and do something to ease the psychic pain that many black men suffer in relative silence. Head looks at this pain and its treatment both up close and in the on-going context of historical and cultural experience. Thus he challenges us in mental health professions and in the larger society to pay attention, too." —Sandra C. Walker, M.D., Psychiatrist and Psychoanalyst

"It is about time an accomplished, well-respected brother talked about their personal struggles with depression—a mental illness that strikes one in five Americans. My hope is this book will bring African American men out of the 'depression closet,' and get the help that will heal them." —Carl C. Bell, M.D., President & C.E.O., Community Mental Health Council

HARLEM MOON
BROADWAY

ALSO BY JOHN HEAD

We Were the Land's:
The Biography of a Homeplace

BLACK MEN
AND
DEPRESSION

Understanding and Overcoming
Depression in Black Men

JOHN HEAD

HARLEM MOON
BROADWAY BOOKS ■ NEW YORK

Published by Harlem Moon, an imprint of Broadway Books, a division of
Random House, Inc.

A hardcover edition of this book was originally published in 2004
by Broadway Books, a division of Random House, Inc., under the title
Standing in the Shadows.

HARLEM MOON, BROADWAY BOOKS, and the HARLEM MOON logo,
depicting a moon and a woman, are trademarks of Random House, Inc.
The figure in the Harlem Moon logo is inspired by a graphic design by
Aaron Douglas (1899–1979).

Visit our website at www.harlemmoon.com

Permissions acknowledgments are on page 210.

First Harlem Moon trade paperback edition published 2005

Book design by Michael Collica

The Library of Congress has cataloged the hardcover as:
Head, John, 1951–
Standing in the shadows : understanding and overcoming depression in
Black men / John Head.— 1st ed.
p. cm.
1. Depression, Mental. 2. African American men—Mental health.
3. Depression in men. I. Title.

RC537.H426 2004
616.85'27'008996073—dc22
2004043625

ISBN 0-7679-1354-X

147429898

To Claire,
the light in the darkness

☒ FOREWORD ☒

No one has written about black men and depression the way John Head has in *Black Men and Depression*. It is long overdue. Depression is terrible in its own right—painful, destructive, isolating, often lethal, and frequently tied to alcohol and drug abuse—but, when it is experienced by black men, the suffering and inequity are compounded. "Black men aren't supposed to need help dealing with depression," writes Head. "It's just one of life's loads that we're supposed to bear, as if we were no more than beasts of burden." Depression, as he points out, is a silent epidemic marked by fear and ignorance: Its damage is even more insidious in those in minority communities, who have had good cause to be skeptical about medical care in general and mental health care in particular.

John Head, who has been a journalist at three of the nation's most respected newspapers, uses his own story of long-unrecognized and untreated depression—a condition that he likens less to Churchill's "black dog" than to a "pack of hounds constantly on his trail"—to illustrate the difficulties in first recognizing, then acknowledging, and finally seeking treatment for depression. He places his own attitudes and behavior in the context of hundreds of years of racism, years that have taken, and continue to take, a terrible toll through the unwillingness to acknowledge "weakness" and a reluctance to take advantage of the tremendous advances in medical and psychological help that are now available. The author discusses the racial as well as medical issues involved in depression; the historic and influential work of Dr. David Satcher, the first black man to be appointed as Surgeon General of the United States, who forcefully advocated for those who suffer from mental illness; and the critical work of Dr. Alvin Poussaint at Harvard, who has done groundbreaking work on the role of race in mental illness and suicide.

Black Men and Depression is a lucid and powerful testament to the life-saving importance of getting treatment for depression. It is also a painful account of how difficult this remains for many people, especially black men. As someone who suffers from mental illness and who also studies and treats it, I found—time and again—how much I learned from John Head. He has written an important book and I wholeheartedly recommend it.

Kay Redfield Jamison, Ph.D.
Professor of Psychiatry
The Johns Hopkins School of Medicine

❆ CONTENTS ❆

ONE

The Silent Epidemic Among Black Men

When I first got the blues, they brought me over on a ship,
Men was standin' over me, and a lot more with a whip.
And ev'rybody wanna know why I sing the blues.

—B. B. King,
"Why I Sing the Blues"

Suppose black men were suffering through an epidemic. What if the disease struck as many as 20 percent of all African American men during their lives, and what if 15 percent of those with the most severe strain of the illness died? Imagine that the disease made men miss work, and made them less motivated and productive when they were on the job. Imagine further that even black men at the top of their professions were affected, rendered less decisive, their judgment impaired. And what if, in an effort to ease the pain of the disease, many African American men medicated themselves with addictive, deadly drugs? What if black families were being destroyed by this illness? What if many of the men suffering from this disease lost hope so completely that they placed little value on human life—theirs or anyone else's? And, finally, what if, while all this was happening, next to nothing was being done to get black men treatment and medications that are 80 percent effective against the disease?

I have no doubt about what would happen. African Americans would be in the streets, charging that black men were the victims of the most vicious form of racism. We would demand action. We would be outraged, and justifiably so.

Yet untreated depression is doing all these things to black men in America. In fact, it probably affects African American men more adversely than it does the general population. "Mental Health: Culture, Race and Ethnicity," the 2001 supplement to the Report on Mental Health by U.S. Surgeon General David Satcher, says that "racial and ethnic minorities collectively experience a greater disability burden from mental illness than do whites."

The release of Dr. Satcher's original Report on Mental Health in 1999 was a landmark moment for America. This was the first comprehensive report on the state of the nation's mental health issued by America's "physician-in-chief." It is both an inventory of the resources available to promote mental health and treat mental illness, and a call to action to use and improve those resources. It paints a portrait of mental illness, filling the canvas with the faces of America, revealing that the direct and indirect effects of mental illness cut across all the nation's dividing lines, whether race, religion, gender, economic level, or education.

But the supplemental report highlights the disparity that exists for black men in mental health as it does in relation to most health problems. For example, African American men are more likely to live with chronic illnesses—and studies show that living with chronic health problems increases the risk of suffering from depression. In its 2002 report, "The Burden of Chronic Diseases and Their Risk Factors," the federal Centers for Disease Control and Prevention points out that African American men have the highest rates of prostate cancer and hypertension in the world. The report also says black men are twice as likely as white men to develop diabetes, and suffer higher rates of heart disease and obesity. The American Cancer Society's 2003 "Cancer Facts and Figures" found that black men are more than twice as likely as white men to die from prostate cancer. We also are more likely than others to wait until an ailment reaches a serious stage before we seek treatment. According to a report issued by the Congressional Black Caucus Foundation in

2003, men in general are three times less likely than women to visit a doctor, and African American men specifically are less likely than white men to go to a doctor before they are in poor health. This is the case for physical ailments. Factor in the stigma attached to mental illness, and add other barriers that keep us from getting help, and it's easy to see why black men are even less likely to seek treatment for depression.

So, I maintain that what I described above—or worse—is happening to black men. But the nation, including the African American community, is silent. The silence on the subject among blacks is due, in part, to our lack of a vocabulary to talk about depression.

We call depression "the blues" in the black community. We're taught to shrug off this mental state. For many of us, it is not just a fact of life; it is a way of life. When bluesmen wail, "Every day I have the blues" or "It ain't nothing but the blues" or similar words from a thousand songs, they do more than mouth lyrics. They voice a cultural attitude. They state the accepted truth at the heart of their music: Having the blues goes along with being black in America.

In addition, from the time we are young boys, black males have ingrained into us an idea of manhood that requires a silence about feelings, a withholding of emotion, an ability to bear burdens alone, and a refusal to appear weak. The internal pressure to adhere to this concept of masculinity only increases as we confront a society that historically has sought to deny us our manhood.

The internal wall that keeps black men away from psychotherapy adjoins external barriers built just as high, if not higher. Mental health practitioners are overwhelmingly white, with the proportion of black psychiatrists, psychologists, and psychoanalysts estimated at less than 3 percent of the nation's total. This means that even if black men break through self-imposed barriers and seek professional help for mental problems, it may be difficult to find someone with whom they can build the rapport that allows a patient to reveal his most intimate secrets. As Dr. Richard Mouzon, a prominent black clinical psychologist in Atlanta, puts it, "We grow up knowing that it's dangerous to give up too much of yourself to the white man."

There's no denying that access to mental health care is restricted for Americans in general. In private health insurance policies and government medical assistance programs, psychotherapy too often is considered a luxury rather than a medical necessity. It often has been said that in America the only people with a guaranteed right to health care are the inmates of our jails and prisons. That's even truer of mental health care. (Unfortunately, it is a right that is of marginal value; while many African American men receive their first and only treatment for mental illness behind bars, that treatment is apt to be directed at keeping them under control rather than alleviating the effects of their illness.)

Our health care system assures preventive measures and early intervention for mental health problems only to the privileged, just as it does for physical health problems. The disparity is so great in minority communities that, for many, mental illness receives attention only when it reaches a florid stage—in public hospitals' emergency rooms and psychiatric wards—or, worse, in its aftermath, when people with mental illness may end up behind bars and in morgues.

The consequences of untreated mental illness are dire. And the tragedy of the worst outcomes can be no greater than when the disorder is depression, one of the most common and treatable mental illnesses. The disease is painful, potentially fatal, but 80 percent of those who get treatment get better. Yet, quite sadly, only 25 percent of those who need help get it. African American men are especially prone to put ourselves in mortal danger because we readily embrace the belief that we can survive depression by riding out the illness, allowing it to run its course. The internal walls we build to keep out the world, and the walls society builds to isolate us, cut us off from the help we need. So we suffer, and we suffer needlessly.

■ ■ ■

I know that suffering firsthand. I dealt with untreated clinical depression for most of my life—into my forty-fifth year, in fact. Anyone looking at the outlines of my life probably would not believe that. They would say good fortune has followed me. I was born in the small town of Jackson, Georgia, which I remember as a good place to grow up, even in the era of segregation and overt racism. I had an older sister and three younger brothers. My mother raised us alone, having divorced my father when I was about four years old. She gave us so much of herself that I don't ever recall feeling deprived of a father. Her mantra was that all things are possible. She worked long hours as a beautician and pushed us to work hard in school to make sure we were prepared to take advantage of all of life's possibilities.

We lived in town, where we had armies of children our own ages as playmates and friends. Of course, we always had one another, despite the moments of sibling warfare in which opposing parties threatened to banish the other from the household by any means necessary. The summer was my favorite time. We spent much of it on my grandparents' farm. My grandmother showered me with love, and my grandfather taught me to work hard and take pride in even the most menial job.

We all did well at our studies, though one of my teachers early on wrote an evaluation of me that placed me in the category of border-line mentally retarded. She said I did not participate in class and, in fact, seemed unable to respond to simple questions. My mother refused to believe her. She argued that my "problems" were nothing more than shyness and a stammer that made speaking in front of others an embarrassing ordeal. She insisted that I not be held back or in any way separated from my peers as long as I was able to demonstrate adequate skills on paper—which I could.

When I reached the third grade and came under the tough-love tutelage of a teacher named Mrs. Doris Lummus, I began to blossom. I scored above grade level on the first standardized test I took. I gained confidence. The grades on my report card went from mostly F's (that stood for "fair," or average, back then) to mostly G's (for "good") and a few E's (for "excellent"). From that point on, I was blessed with teachers who believed in me and encouraged me to believe in myself. At home, of course, there was always Mom, reinforcing the teachers.

This also was the time of my life that I fell in love with baseball.

There's no getting away from it: I was not much of an athlete. I was neither as strong nor as fast as my teammates. But I threw myself into the game with a dedication far beyond the most unbridled youthful enthusiasm. During the summer, I persuaded my brothers to get up with me at dawn and hike down to the baseball field for practice sessions. They hit ground ball after ground ball to me at my shortstop position. I fielded and threw to first base, often wildly; the balls were wet and slick after rolling through dewy grass. In the afternoon there were regular team practices, each of which I approached with an intensity that others would have reserved for championship games. Back home, late into the night, I practiced swing after swing with a leaded bat I had fashioned. I swung half right-handed and half left-handed, so I could become as great a switch-hitter as Mickey Mantle. Then I took the bat and held it one-handed and at arm's length, flexing it up and down so I could develop wrists as strong and quick as Hank Aaron's.

I had a reputation around town as a baseball maniac. Looking back with a better understanding of how my brain works, I believe it would be more accurate to say that baseball brought out my manic side. That state of single-mindedness, boundless energy, and belief that any goal was within my reach took me beyond the limits of my mediocre physical talents. It got me through an Atlanta Braves tryout camp. More than two hundred players showed up, all determined to live their dream. Only two were invited to the Braves' minor league spring training camp. I was one of the lucky two. It wasn't until I got down to West Palm Beach, Florida, and practiced and played alongside the likes of Dusty Baker and other future Major League stars that I learned I was not going to be a professional baseball player. For a while, though, I stood on a manicured field, looked up at palm trees, and smelled the scent of the ocean carried on a mild breeze. And I knew I was in a place millions of boys dream of reaching, but where very few actually arrive.

That is just one highlight of what many would consider a charmed life. I was the first in my family to finish college, graduating with honors from Georgia State University with a degree in journalism. My good luck with teachers had continued. One of my professors at GSU was a wonderful man named George Greiff. He took me under his wing; he became my mentor and a father figure for me. We stayed close until his death, more than thirty years after I met him. George not only taught me what I needed to know to become a journalist, he also used his contacts to help me get my first job after graduation. Classmates who could match my talents struggled to find jobs in the field, but I left school with a job waiting for me at one of the nation's leading newspapers, the *Detroit Free Press.*

At the time of my move to Detroit in the summer of 1973, I had never spent more than a few days anywhere outside of Georgia. Experiencing a place so culturally different from the one in which I grew up was exciting to me. New friends at the *Free Press* took great delight in sharing the joys of Detroit's ethnic neighborhoods and restaurants. I was a twenty-two-year-old single man living in a place where almost everything was new to me. And 1973 was an especially exciting time to be a black journalist in urban America. That year, Tom Bradley was elected the first African American mayor of Los Angeles; Maynard Jackson—for whom I would eventually work—won the same post in Atlanta; and Coleman Young would make the same kind of history in Detroit only a few months after I arrived in the Motor City. This small-town Georgia boy was like a dry sponge taking its first dip in water. I soaked it all up.

Discovering the joys of Detroit's spicy stew of cultures was one thing. Surviving the city's climate was quite another. The seemingly nine-month-long northern winter did me in. My coworkers took bets on what I would wear next in an attempt to keep warm. Finally, as a snow and ice storm hit Detroit on April 1 (I considered this the city's April Fool's present to me), I packed my car and drove south. I headed home to Georgia, where I had a standing job offer from the *Atlanta Journal,* the city's afternoon daily.

In all, I spent more than twenty years at the *Journal-Constitution* (the morning *Constitution* and afternoon *Journal* became one newspaper in a years-long metamorphosis that ended in 2001). My time at the *AJC* was accumulated in four prodigal-son episodes in which

I left the paper and came back. Interspersed were stints as press secretary to Mayor Jackson; as a lecturer in the journalism department at Georgia State University, my alma mater; as a reporter, national desk assistant editor, and Atlanta bureau chief for *USA Today*; and as a latter-day bohemian driving around the country in a VW camper while trying to write the great American novel.

As I've said, many would argue I've led a life in which a long series of good luck and accomplishments has been strung together. In my mind, however, there was one thread running through all the good things in my life: I didn't deserve them. I thought of myself as a phony, an imposter who was certain to be found out in the end. Any praise directed at me was a generous lie. I was destined for spectacular failure, but mere fate for some reason kept preventing it from happening. I believed in my heart that eventually I would fall and get what I really deserved.

Racism no doubt fed these feelings. Yet there was more than my reaction to racism at play. Like any other black child in America, I'd begun learning how to cope with racism as soon as I understood how things would be stacked against me in life. The people around me drummed into me the coping skills they had learned. At school, my teachers told me that if I ever got a chance to compete with whites I'd better be twice as good as they in order to have any chance of coming out on top. If I'd been someone whose mind could latch onto the positive, this kind of indoctrination might have inoculated me against racism. But my mind didn't always work that way. My brain's circuits were connected to life's negative battery terminal.

So racism created a double whammy for me: I felt the pressure of the high expectations of those who cared about me, while at the same time I feared the fulfillment of the prophesies of doom made by those who hated me because of the color of my skin.

The emotional lows that resulted from my view of the world and the way I fit in it—or, rather, didn't fit—came and went. There were moments of justified euphoria, as when, at the age of twenty-seven, I sold my first short story to a magazine. Minutes after opening the acceptance letter, I was on my bicycle racing through Atlanta's

Piedmont Park, so fast that the rushing air pushed tears from the corners of my eyes. I wanted to shout for joy and let the sound follow in my wake for all to hear. Selling that short story—actually knowing that someone was willing to pay for the right to publish a product of my imagination—opened the door to a new world for me. It was a world about which I had dreamed for most of my life, ever since my second-grade teacher picked my story as the best in the class. She read it aloud, and my classmates laughed and clapped at the end. I was hooked. The simple selling of a short story was enough to make me feel that I had begun my climb to the top of the writing world.

But I paid dearly for such emotional highs. They made the lows far more frequent, more devastating. The layers of fear, anxiety, and doubt that pressed down on me seemed impossible to escape. Everything was a struggle. Performing the simplest task at work was a challenge. On weekends, getting out of bed was an act of extraordinary willpower. Some weekends I couldn't summon the energy to throw back the sheets and get up, except to get food or drag myself to the couch to watch TV—the self-medication in a box that temporarily numbed my mind and stilled the demons inside it.

The only thing that made the lows bearable was the realization that they wouldn't last forever, even if it seemed they would. Some were longer than others, but they all eventually ended. I would revert to my baseball attitude. "Suck it up," I scolded myself. "Stop whining and feeling sorry for yourself. Get back in the game. And if you're going to play, hustle like it all means something."

I was able to psych myself back up, even allowing a few of those euphoric moments to wash over me. I just needed to be strong and not give in to the weakness. These mental gymnastics worked so many times, I thought they always would. But there came a time when my descent into the slippery-sided pit of depression continued unabated for months.

It was during my year in Detroit that I first plunged to emotional depths so low that I and the people around me could tell something was seriously wrong. Thus began my recurring bouts of psychic free fall, followed by periods of emotional buoyancy that brought me back up. I would reach an even-keel baseline and sometimes rise to a peak of euphoria. Once it started in earnest, this cycle repeated itself unabated for more than twenty years.

I left the snow and ice behind when I fled Detroit on that April Fool's Day in 1974. But the depression that chilled my spirit followed me all the way back to Atlanta. Winston Churchill described depression as his "black dog." For me, it was like a pack of hounds constantly on my trail. There were times when I got far enough out in front of these dogs of depression that I could barely hear them baying in the distance. There were other times, however, when they snapped at my heels, even clamped their jaws on me and pulled me down.

Just like any other untreated chronic illness, my depression got progressively worse with the passage of time. The emotional highs became fewer and further between. I dived to the lows at dizzying speeds and hit bottom with soul-shattering force. My depression robbed me of the ability to enjoy life. There was much I should have enjoyed in the early 1990s, as I entered my forties. I had three sons, to whom I was determined to be a good father. (When my middle son, Gabriel, was born, I became the first man at the *Atlanta Journal-Constitution* to request and receive paternity leave, in order to stay home with him for his first three months.) My second marriage—to Claire Broome, a smart, beautiful woman and a wonderful mother to our children—was at five years and counting. Physically, I was in excellent health, playing competitive tennis and getting plenty of exercise to stay in shape. There wasn't a whole lot more I wanted out of my job, having become a member of the editorial board and a columnist for the *Constitution*.

Clearly, this should have been a time for me to savor the fruits of a good life. Instead, it was the time when my unhappiness became more and more evident.

Family, friends, coworkers, and others who cared about me tried to help. Someone actually told me to "turn it over to God." But I hadn't been inside a church in years, other than for weddings and funerals. Others urged me to do more "fun" things, such as go to parties, visit nightclubs, or go dancing—things I would rarely or never do even in a state of sky-high euphoria. One well-intentioned friend told me I just needed to "get back that old John Head enthusiasm," as if my more upbeat persona could be turned on and off at the flick of a switch.

I rejected and resented all the advice, the good along with the bad. People couldn't figure out how to reach me. They couldn't fathom that the more desperate my situation became, the less I was willing to accept help of any kind.

At work, I was barely functional. I was unproductive and sloppy. I had nightmares of being fired for missing the deadline on an important story or for making a mistake that held the newspaper up to ridicule. I craved sleep throughout the day, no matter how much I'd slept the night before. In meetings I had trouble staying awake, much less paying attention.

Things were even worse at home. I had no enthusiasm for family activities. My interactions with my three sons too often consisted of screaming fits, often for little or no reason. I roamed the house like a summer storm cloud, brooding and prone to explode with thunder and lightning, a source of danger even from the emotional distance at which I always kept my family.

The worst part of feeling so miserable was that I believed I was spreading the misery to my family, like some infectious disease. I thought I was never going to feel better; I knew with certainty that things would only get worse. I could not bear the thought that this was the image of me my sons would grow up with and always remember. I barely remember my own father. The most vivid memory I have of him is of a shouting match between him and my mother. He had left a mason jar of moonshine in the refrigerator. I found it and, thinking it was lemonade, took a gulp and threw up. That's the snapshot of my father in my mind. I feared my son's minds would hold long-running movies of me as a sullen, resentful, and angry man who did not show them the love they craved.

And my marriage was falling apart. If anyone had asked me why,

I couldn't have given a reason that made any sense. I would have only said that I was to blame. Knowing what I know now, I believe my depression definitely played a role. Even in its mildest phases, my depression was like a diluted acid eating way at the edges of the marriage. My irritability, my lack of interest in or energy for doing things just for the fun of them, and my other symptoms were shrinking any chance we had for commonality and a caring bond. As the depression got worse, the acid became more corrosive. It seeped into the center of the marriage and began dissolving it from the inside out. The inability to communicate, the emotional shutdown, the loss of intimacy—these manifestations of my depression threatened the core of our marriage. The loss of intimacy may be depression's most destructive impact on a marriage. The intimacy to which I refer isn't just the sexual relationship, although that is an aspect of it. I'm talking about the general, wide-ranging intimacy between couples. It is the sense of togetherness, the sharing that binds a man and a woman together as they are bound to no others.

One partner's depression breaks the most basic bonds of loving relationships, while inviting the formation of competing relationships. (More about that later.) The breach brought on by a violation of the trust between two people is difficult to repair under any circumstances. The way depression cripples a relationship means the repair work is nearly impossible unless the depression is addressed.

I had no faith in marriage when I was in the grip of depression. I had no faith in any kind of loving relationship. Committing myself to someone, handing my heart over to her, was difficult and scary. Why put in the emotional effort, if I believed no good would ever come of it? I was convinced that such a relationship would not make me happy, because I knew I was destined to live a life of unhappiness.

And everything was made worse because of the indecisiveness depression spawned. How could I make a decision when I believed in my heart of hearts that any choice would be the wrong one? Stay in the marriage and do nothing more than spread my misery to my family. Leave the marriage and remain lonely and unloved—and guilt-ridden at becoming the kind of father my father had been.

Claire and I were constantly on the verge of divorce, because I'd insist that I wanted out of the marriage, only to pull back and insist that the marriage could be saved. It must have been maddening for Claire, being the string that got wound up in my emotional yo-yo.

One day I told Claire that I had found an apartment and was moving out. When she asked me why, my only explanation was "You'll all be better off without me around." She said the boys needed me and would miss me. I responded that I would still be a part of their lives, but I didn't want to be the constant negative force I had become for them.

There was little discussion once my mind finally seemed to be made up. Claire's last words to me were ones she had uttered in a pleading voice many times before: "Get help."

Claire believed in the benefits of professional therapy. I was resistant to the idea. It was foreign to me, in fact. My inclination had always been to keep my problems to myself. This is common among men in general, and especially among black men. It is central to our refusal to seek the help we need. We don't want to be questioned about what we're feeling. We'd rather silently question our need to get help when we struggle with our emotions. "What's the value in talking about my feelings," I thought, "and talking about them to a complete stranger, at that?"

My attitude about this didn't apply only to psychotherapy. Claire and I made several attempts at marriage counseling. It would be more accurate to say that Claire made the attempts. I was an unwilling participant, if what I did could truly be called participation. My depression surely was part of the problem. I didn't see the value in trying to make things better; I had no hope that things ever would be better.

But even when I was in my most positive frame of mind, I had an aversion to the process of therapy or counseling. The concept of learning to communicate and to make a relationship work through role-playing, exercises, and other techniques seemed forced and unnatural to me. None of it appealed to me in any of its various forms. I remember a work-related retreat I had to take part in. It involved lots of role-playing, lots of lessons in communication and problem-solving skills. When it was over, one of my coworkers who had not taken part in the retreat asked me how it went. "It was like being in a failing marriage with two hundred people and going through counseling with all of them at the same time," I said.

That I felt that way about counseling must have been frustrating for Claire. And her frustration level rose with my failure to make it clear whether I believed anything would save the marriage. People make life-altering decisions in the hope that any change will be for the better. Again, I lacked hope and therefore had little motivation to make decisions.

Given my attitude and history, it is no wonder Claire accepted my decision to leave: even if she believed it was the wrong decision, at least it was a decision.

The leasing agent called the unit I rented a balcony apartment. That didn't mean there was a balcony outside. The balcony was inside. The apartment had two levels. Downstairs were a small living room and a kitchen. Upstairs, where the balcony overlooked the living room, there was just over half as much floor space—just room enough for a small bedroom and bath.

As small as the apartment was, it seemed to be more space than I needed. It was little more than the place where I spent my time when I wasn't at work. I had the sense that my personal space in the world was getting smaller, collapsing in on me. I was a sort of black hole. I needed no space. Besides that, the upstairs bedroom was more or less useless to me. I seldom felt like climbing the stairs just to get into bed. Most often I flopped down on the couch and slept there. That was where I could get my anesthetic doses of TV.

I lived in the apartment for six months. During that time, I was the only person who set foot inside it. I didn't want visitors. I had a telephone and an answering machine. In those six months I got two or three calls that weren't solicitations or wrong numbers. All the calls that were actually for me were from a tennis buddy who lived nearby. My love of the game motivated me enough to go out and play matches with him two or three times a week, even though I never won and left the court angry and frustrated.

The apartment had become a cave where I could isolate myself from the rest of the world. I was safe from all the advice givers and all those who tried to cheer me up. I wanted to escape their expressions of concern. I especially remember the people who could read in my face a mixture of sorrow, pain, and anger. Some of them approached me with good-natured smiles, signaling that what they were about to say was not serious, that they were setting the stage for the joke. They walked up to me and asked, "Who died?" I was in a perpetually somber state of mind. I had a serious answer to their comic question, but I never used it. I wanted to look into their smiling faces and reply, "Nobody yet. But I will."

If any man of medicine tried to explain the mental state of the first Africans to arrive in America as slaves—or, for that matter, the condition of mind that drove some to throw themselves into the ocean during the Middle Passage—his diagnosis is lost to history. But there can be little doubt that it would have been a misdiagnosis, for to observe that blacks had psyches susceptible to damage by traumatic experiences just as whites did would have violated the primary tenet of the "peculiar institution" of slavery: that the Africans brought here in bondage were not fully human. On that day when the first slave ship docked more than three centuries ago, the most humane among those involved in the importation of blacks as slaves to these shores would have considered the Africans the unfortunate descendants of Cain, fated by God to be hewers of wood and drawers of water. Others of less kind inclination saw the new arrivals as no different from any other stock animal needed to make plantations productive. It's no wonder, then, if no one who examined those first Africans on American soil—checking their teeth and limbs to ensure that they were sound of body and fit for work—gave any thought to their mental health, much less created any historical record of it.

What *is* recorded in history is that the study of the mind has not been kind to blacks in general and to black men in particular. From the earliest days, when it was little more than guesswork and super-stition, this medical discipline was determined to demonstrate the mental inferiority of blacks. Belief that four bodily fluids, called humors, controlled human disposition was widespread. The dark humor, black bile, was blamed for the most negative mental states. Thus dark skin was associated with a tendency toward "dark" moods. Slaves who were unhappy with their lot in life were said to suffer from "sable melancholy." A slave who ran away from his master had a form of madness called "drapetomania," also known as "neurotic restlessness."

Given the ideas about race prevalent among white Americans at the time, it's not surprising that more thought was given to describ-ing what mental disorders caused blacks to resist slavery than was given to identifying mental disorders that slavery might cause in blacks. Dr. Benjamin Rush, a signer of the Declaration of Indepen-dence and arguably the new nation's most prominent physician, did note the emotional harm slavery could do. Rush is credited with identifying insanity as a disease of the mind rather than a matter of demonic possession. In 1812, he published *Observations and Inquiries upon the Diseases of the Mind,* considered the first psychi-atric textbook printed in the United States; his efforts to reform mental health care earned him the title "the Father of American Psychiatry." Rush was also an ardent abolitionist. In 1813, he wrote that "Africans become insane, we are told, in some instances, soon after they enter upon the toils of perpetual slavery in the West Indies." (The West Indies was one of the last places on earth where enslaved Africans wanted to find themselves. Its system of bondage was especially brutal, and American planters found it a convenient dumping ground for troublesome slaves. Shipping a slave to the West Indies was like sentencing him to death. George Washington was one of the slave owners who did this, as he recounted in a letter describing the arrangements he made to rid himself of a slave who kept running away.)

To this day, Americans focus on the physical brutality of slavery while mostly ignoring the psychological trauma. In truth, the emotional carnage slavery wrought among blacks may have been worse. Consider how having families broken up for sale sent out ripples of psychic pain that reverberated through generations. In Toni Morrison's acclaimed novel *Beloved,* a woman kills her child rather than allowing her to be subjected to a life of slavery. Such stories are inspired by actual events that echo through history. In 1745, for example, a South Carolina slave called Kate was accused of killing her child. She was judged insane. Her case ultimately led the South Carolina assembly to require each county's parishes to establish funds to pay for confinement of insane slaves.

Benjamin Rush was ahead of his time in some aspects of his thinking on the health of black Americans. In other aspects, however, he was merely a man of his times. He believed blacks suffered from "negritude," a condition that could only be cured by finding some way to turn blacks into whites. Even as he campaigned to establish institutions to care for the insane, he believed blacks and whites should be treated in segregated facilities. With friends like Rush fighting for African Americans on the mental health front, it's easy to imagine the deep-seated hostility of their enemies.

Rather than consider that slavery fostered mental disorders in blacks, some saw the system as a boon to the mental stability of slaves. Louisiana's Dr. Samuel Cartwright, considered at the time a leading authority on the medical conditions of slaves, wrote in 1851 that northern doctors who saw evidence that slavery caused blacks to suffer emotionally had gotten things backward. "They ignorantly attribute the symptoms [of emotional disorders in slaves] to the debasing influence of slavery on the mind without considering that [blacks] who have never been in slavery, or their fathers before them, are the most afflicted, and the latest from the slave-holding South the least," Cartwright said. "The disease is the natural offspring of Negro liberty—the liberty to be idle, to wallow in filth, and to indulge in improper food and drinks." In other words, it's being free that drives blacks insane.

Even after Cartwright and other practitioners of early forms of psychology developed what they called scientific, objective bases for their conclusions, African Americans continued to see evidence of bias against them. From the nineteenth century's crude measuring of skulls to "prove" that blacks had smaller brains and therefore were less intelligent than whites, to the 1990s' sophisticated use of statistical data and graphs in *The Bell Curve* to demonstrate the futility of trying to "improve black intelligence" through social programs, blacks have seen little benefit in the science of the psyche.

That's only one of the reasons the African American community's skepticism about mental health care has risen to the level of hostility. The church's central role in black culture fed the belief that the only way to soothe a troubled mind was to have a talk with God, either through pastoral counseling or directly through prayer.

Then there is mistrust of "experimental" medicine in the African American community, stemming from instances of blacks being used as human guinea pigs, including the decades-long Tuskegee study in which black men were denied the most effective treatment for syphilis so that doctors could observe the devastating course of the disease. This and similar episodes of medical research may have been isolated incidents, completely out of character for the American health care system. Yet their effect on how blacks view that system, and on our willingness to use its resources, is widespread. For example, as the 2003 influenza season approached, the federal Centers for Disease Control and Injury Prevention reported on the percentage of people sixty-five and older—the group at highest risk of death from the disease—who receive flu shots. Surveys showed blacks are less likely to get the inoculations than whites and Hispanics.

Given our history and our attitudes toward health care, it's no surprise that the relationship between African Americans and psychotherapy has "progressed," at best, to the level of Ms. Distrust meeting Mr. Indifference on a blind date. Still, we should have come further. As a group, mental health practitioners are social progressives. They are not only healers of the subconscious; they are doctors with consciences. Their premise is that those whose behavior or way of thinking is outside society's norms are not necessarily weak or evil. They emphasize the therapeutic over the punitive. And they believe rehabilitation is almost always possible. Their concern is with those who suffer life's traumas and become the outsiders, the ostracized, the despised, the alienated, the feared. The field, on its face, would seem suited to delve deeply into the consequences of the black male experience in America. But because of the way our nation's health care system operates, the profession doesn't deal with those consequences enough.

The painful truth is that African American men are cut off from the mental health care system by barriers that are often insurmountable. Without a doubt, some are self-imposed. The stigma placed on mental illness and on seeking mental health treatment is strong among blacks, although the attitude certainly isn't unique to the black community. Prejudice against people with mental illness is readily apparent in our society, and psychotherapy comes under suspicion in many quarters. The mainstream media's portrayals of people with mental illness are overwhelmingly negative. The news media are most likely to mention mental illness in connection with a violent crime, whether or not there is evidence of a connection between the mental disorder and the violence. There aren't many articles written about the people who get better thanks to mental health treatment. In fact, television viewers and moviegoers seldom see a happy outcome when mental illness makes its way into scripts; those characters usually get worse. The psychologists, psychiatrists, and psychoanalysts who appear on television and movie screens are as likely to be evil and manipulative as they are to be the healers they're trained to be. More positive portrayals pop up in television shows such as *The Sopranos* and movies such as *A Beautiful Mind* and *Antwone Fisher*, but these remain the exceptions in a tide of media negativity.

Media presentations of mental illness among minorities are even more rare and more problematic. This is especially true when it comes to black men and mental illness. If you see a news account of a black man suffering from psychological problems, chances are the story involves violence, as was the case with Colin Ferguson, who in 1993 killed six people during a shooting spree on a Long Island commuter train. More recently, the inability of the boxer Mike Tyson to control his anger has made him the media's poster boy for emotional disorders among black men. And I would hazard a guess that nine times out of ten, a mentally ill black man portrayed in a movie or a television show is homeless and suffering from schizophrenia. The script will call for him to be violent or to behave in a bizarrely comical way. He will neither want treatment nor have treatment offered to him. When the final scene fades to black, his condition will be unchanged.

I can recall only one case in which a black male character suffering from a mental illness seeks help and remains highly functional. That's Talcott Garland, the narrator and hero of Stephen L. Carter's best-selling novel *The Emperor of Ocean Park*. In fact, the rare novel, movie, or TV drama whose plot involves a mentally ill black man's encounter with psychotherapy is more likely than not to present a negative outcome, with the treatment either having no effect or somehow making things worse.

Meanwhile, real-life critics such as the Church of Scientology attack psychiatry and psychotropic drugs as the causes of mental problems rather than as solutions. Scientology, in fact, specifically seeks to stoke mistrust of psychotherapy among blacks, portraying psychiatrists as tools of racism.

It's not as though we need anyone to give us a push in that general direction, with respect to the black community's attitudes toward those with mental illnesses and the physicians who treat them. A National Institute of Mental Health survey found that 60 percent of African Americans view depression as a weakness rather than as an illness. Dr. Quentin "Ted" Smith, a professor of clinical psychiatry at Atlanta's Morehouse School of Medicine, spoke of this during a forum at the Jimmy Carter Presidential Center in 2003: Asked about African American attitudes toward depression, Dr. Smith said, "Sometimes it seems people would rather have an illness like cancer than have depression."

Maynard Jackson was one of the smartest, most erudite men I've ever known. My admiration for him grew while I worked as his press secretary during his mayoralty. After serving three terms and returning to private life, Maynard decided to write a book. I was honored that he asked me to help him with it. Unfortunately, Maynard died before the book was finished.

I met with him and discussed the book the week before he died. Near the end of our three-hour meeting, Maynard said to me, "I've got to make a tough decision about whether or how I address my father's breakdown in this book."

Maynard's father, Maynard Jackson, Sr., suffered what was referred to as a "nervous breakdown" when Maynard was a teenager. The episode, during which the elder Jackson was hospitalized, is chronicled in *Where Peachtree Meets Sweet Auburn,* the excellent book by Gary Pomerantz that includes a history of Maynard's family. Maynard said the book presents an accurate portrayal of what happened, but that there was much more to tell, including Maynard's own deep-seated feelings at the time.

I urged Maynard to write about it, and not because it would provide compelling material for the book, even though it certainly would. "Maynard, this is exactly what the book I'm writing is about," I said. "It's about mental illness and the black community. One of the things I've come to believe while working on the book is that more black people need to speak out about mental illness. We need to talk about our own experiences. That's one of the best ways to make a difference."

"I know," Maynard said. "I have to think about it in a number of ways, including about how I felt about it at the time. The thing I remember most is how embarrassed I felt for my father when it happened. And to this day, I'm ashamed of having felt ashamed."

Maynard didn't get the chance to think about it. I like to think he would have worked things out in his mind and decided to write about it in his book. I believe he would have written with his usual eloquence and humanity. And I believe he would have made a difference.

More often than not, we lack the communal vocabulary to talk meaningfully about mental illness. In the black community of the small Georgia town where I grew up, someone was either "in his right mind" or had "lost his mind." There were no words for the netherworld in between, where people struggle every day with depression and other disorders. And there certainly was no concept of mental health care, of a way to prevent people from "losing" their minds or to restore minds that had been lost. The closest thing to mental health treatment in our vocabulary was "going to Milledgeville," Milledgeville being the city where Georgia's state "insane asylum" was located. For many years it was an institution in the classic "snake pit" mold, a facility where conditions were so bad that an exposé of what went on inside its walls earned Jack Nelson, then a reporter for the *Atlanta Constitution,* a Pulitzer Prize in 1960.

The idea that people might be functioning in their day-to-day lives and yet still pay someone to treat their emotional problems was outright bizarre to us. In fact, we thought it was only in the white world that such a thing might happen. "Black folks can't *afford* to be crazy," we would say.

The mind-set that allows us to visualize a "Whites Only" sign on the doorway to depression and other mental illnesses wasn't then and isn't now limited to black folks in small towns. At a banquet I attended in the spring of 2003, I sat next to one of the living legends of the civil rights movement. He labored on the front lines of the fight for black equality for most of his adult life. Always known for his intellect and sophistication, he eventually became a man of wealth and a power in the political and corporate world. While we chatted, the fact that I was writing a book came up.

"What's it about?" he asked.

"It's about black men and depression," I said. "One of the main points I'm trying to make is that depression is a problem that just isn't talked about in the black community."

"You know, we didn't have any of that stuff until after integration," he said.

I didn't quite know how to respond to that. I just gave him one of those smiles that say, "You're kidding, right?"

He picked up on it immediately. "I'm serious!" he exclaimed. "Dead serious. Just think about it."

Well, just thinking about it, I can't recall ever hearing of anyone in my hometown being referred to as having a mental disorder. There *were* people of whom it was said that they "lost their mind" or "had a nervous breakdown," but these either quickly recovered or were "gone to Milledgeville." As for people who actually lived among us as they wrestled with emotional demons, they were unnamed or nonexistent.

But they did exist, of course. We knew their names, but we didn't know the names of their disorders. I remember a boy who was about my age and who lived next door to us for a while. He couldn't speak; the only sounds that came out of his mouth were guttural grunts. People said he was "slow" or "simple-minded." Yet it was clear something more was tormenting him. He had "fits," when he burst into uncontrollable anger. People would hold him, restrain him, and try to calm him. Sometimes his family kept him locked inside. Once, when he was in his teens, he came out of the house naked, his grunts rapid and almost as high-pitched as screams. I can only guess now what he suffered from. Was it schizophrenia? Was he voiceless except for the voices inside his head? I don't have the answers. Back when I knew him, I didn't even know to ask the questions.

There was a white teenager I knew. He had a habit of constantly touching things. His hands were always fluttering toward something, like butterflies flitting around flowers. And he was as skittish as a deer; he always seemed ready to take flight from something. Near panic seized him if anyone said or did anything remotely threatening. Some kids delighted in getting this kind of reaction from him. He was a bully's dream. Could he have had an obsessive-compulsive disorder, along with his obvious anxiety?

An old black man walked the streets of downtown and the town's neighborhoods carrying on a conversation with someone who wasn't there. He always had a croaker sack with something heavy inside slung over his shoulder. Parents told their children the old man would put them in his sack and take them away if they were bad. They created a legend for him, but they didn't try to explain his behavior.

The way my hometown treated people with mental illness is probably the way such people were treated in many small towns. Most times we went out of our way to accommodate them, to make allowances that enabled their world to coexist with ours. Some we ignored, or tried our best to. Perhaps a few were hidden away. What we didn't do, as far as I know, was get them the professional help they needed.

      ■ ■ ■

African American men who suffer from depression pay a high price for failing to deal with the disease. We are aided in that failure by the ignorance and neglect of a nation that has yet to confront, or even to measure, the scope of the problem, though signs of that problem are everywhere. For that neglect, America also is paying a high price.

Violence, substance abuse, irresponsible sexual conduct, abandonment of families, lack of initiative, low self-esteem—these are among the "pathologies" ticked off in diagnoses of what ails African American society. Black males are blamed for spreading these conditions, for infecting our communities. The "treatment" this country favors is to quarantine us (in jails and prisons) or to wait for the conditions to run their courses in us, the carriers, until we die out.

If we're interested in solving these social problems, we must accept some of the worst behaviors among black men not only as the result of metaphorical illnesses, but as symptoms of a very real one. Clinical depression is that illness.

Clinical depression—depression for which medical treatment is called for—is technically named "major depressive disorder" in the latest edition of the American Psychiatric Association's *Diagnostic and Statistical Manual of Mental Disorders,* Fourth Edition (DSM-IV). According to the DSM-IV, major depressive disorder can be diagnosed if, within a two-week period, a patient exhibits at least five of nine symptoms. The nine symptoms range from being in a depressed mood for most of the day to attempting suicide. Symptoms vary widely within that range. In fact, they can even contradict each other. An inability to sleep can be a sign of depression. So can sleeping too much. Some people who are depressed lose weight. Others gain weight. But there are two symptoms that have to be among the five needed to make a diagnosis: "The cardinal symptoms of major depressive disorder are depressed mood and loss of interest or pleasure," the Surgeon General's Report on Mental Health says.*

The Surgeon General's report says that about 7 percent of Americans suffer from mood disorders over the course of a year, with depression being the leading mood disorder. It also estimates that between 15 and 20 percent of Americans will suffer from major depression during their lifetime.

The disease is insidious. On an individual, person-by-person level, the depth of the damage it does is most evident among African American men who are succeeding—those of us who are "making it" by society's standards. Depression denies our families and us the enjoyment of our achievements. It erodes our ability to nurture our children and to teach them—and, by example, all children—the things that got us through. It distorts our thinking so much that we refuse to accept our accomplishments as evidence of who we have become, and instead embrace society's negative stereotypes of us. Even if we achieve high status and accumulate power, as black men with depression we suffer unseen and unheard. We are standing in the shadows, invisible men to the nation at large, to our own communities, to our families, and even to ourselves.

Worst of all, depression destroys the very things that allow us to lift ourselves up—our belief in ourselves and our belief in the possibility of a brighter future.

When we consider its impact in terms of sheer numbers and the negative consequences for our communities and the nation, depres-

---

*See chapter 11, A Guide to Resources for Fighting Depression (page 193), for a full description of the symptoms of clinical depression.

sion clearly does the most damage among the masses of black men who already are on the margins of society. Depression can tip them over the edge. The ripple effects of the devastation spread throughout American society.

This book is not an attempt to offer depression as the explanation for every act of violence, every crime, and all the irresponsible conduct of every black man in America. Nobody would argue that depression is the *only* reason too many of us abandon our families, fail to support our children, fall into drug abuse, wind up behind bars, kill each other. No one should make the case that a diagnosis of depression should be tantamount to an act of absolution for African American men, an apologia that pronounces all of us mentally ill and blameless for our conduct.

This book *is* a plea for black men with depression to walk out of the shadows, to stop suffering in silence, and a plea for our people to remove the stigma attached to mental illness, that is a gag stuffed into our mouths. This book urges the criminal justice and social services systems to seriously consider depression's effect on the behavior of African American men, and to factor in that effect in formulating policies aimed at changing the behavior. This book argues that our culture and our history in this country make black men especially vulnerable when depression strikes. We are less likely to seek the help of mental health practitioners. When we do seek help, we are more likely to be misdiagnosed, improperly medicated, and/or offered treatment that lacks cultural sensitivity and therefore is less effective than it could be. For me, the evidence is clear, in published research, interviews with experts on psychotherapy, and in my own experience dealing with depression.

I imagine what I say on these pages won't please everyone. Some may believe I'm adding to the so-called culture of victimhood that they claim afflicts blacks. Quite the contrary: My purpose is to convince black men to stop being victims of a disease we can fight and defeat. Some may see an attempt to raise awareness of depression in black men as an example of what they derisively call the Disease-of-the-Month Club mentality that turns illnesses into fads. To those critics I say this: It's possible that any attention focused on depression in black men could go the way of fads, fading away as the public's short attention span wanders off to other things. But depression and the damage it does are not fads; they will not fade away. The longer we do nothing about depression in black men, the longer it will be with us.

The issues surrounding depression in African American men are important beyond the impact on our families, our communities, and ourselves. They are important to the nation as a whole. Our country's health care system is flawed. Those flaws are writ large in the system's inability to adequately address depression in black men. If it cannot deal with a problem when the need is so obvious and the benefits of providing solutions are so enormous, the system reveals itself as not merely flawed, but possibly broken beyond repair. When he served as U.S. Surgeon General, Dr. David Satcher often said the U.S. Public Health Service is guided by a variation on this theme. "To the extent that we respond to the needs of the most vulnerable," Satcher said, "we do the most to promote the health of the nation."

More than three centuries removed from the landing of the first slaves on these shores, Americans look back aghast at the physical suffering African Americans' ancestors endured, and at the slave-owning society's refusal to acknowledge that suffering, much less make any attempt to ease it. Yet two of the essential questions that could have been asked more than three hundred years ago remain unanswered: Will the psychological suffering of African Americans be acknowledged? What will be done to ease it? Our society has changed and progressed in ways that would have been unimaginable to either the slavers or the slaves of those days. But America's failure to address the damage that depression does to African American men is rooted, in part, in prejudice and stigma that date all the way back to the docking of that first slave ship. Black men aren't supposed to need help dealing with depression. It's just one of life's loads that we're supposed to bear, as if we were no more than beasts of burden.

■ TWO ■

The Roots of Depression
in Black Men

I'm so forlorn, life's just a thorn, my heart is torn, why was I born?
What did I do to be so black and blue?

—Andy Razaf,
"(What Did I Do to Be So) Black and Blue"

The experts know a lot about depression. Because it is one of the most prevalent mental disorders, it's one of the most thoroughly researched. Scientists have made impressive strides in recent years toward understanding causes and cures, if by cures we mean treatments that bring about sustained improvements and control the illness rather than eliminate it.

Yet our understanding of depression in African American men is characterized by how much we don't know, and by how much of what we think we know is suspect. Research is insufficient to answer some of the most basic questions about depression in black men. For example, the currently accepted conclusion that the rate of depression in African American men is roughly equivalent to that for whites is wide open to debate. It is true that no studies have shown higher rates of depression in black men, but this may be because comparative demographic studies are few. The limited statistical studies comparing rates of depression in African American men and in other groups are suspect for the same reason that surveys showing greater rates of depression in women than in men may not be completely reliable. There definitely are differences between men and women based on biology and social circumstances that place women at greater risk of depression. But the accepted disparity between the rate of depression in men and the rate in women is probably skewed, because women are more willing to seek help and accept a diagnosis of depression, while men tend to refuse to seek help at all. Black men's resistance to seeking help and their lack of access to mental health care make the likely discrepancy between the number who are diagnosed with depression and the number who actually suffer from it even greater. The few studies of the prevalence of depression in African American men report that 8 to 10 percent of us suffer serious depression in a year.

The unhappy era when psychotherapists and mental health researchers mostly ignored the issues surrounding mental illness in African Americans and other minorities could not survive the 1960s and the civil rights movement. By the 1970s, it was widely accepted that the problems of mental illness, and the solutions to those problems, were the same for minorities as for whites. That was a huge step forward. Recognition that cultural differences affect why people suffer from mental illness and how they should be treated took hold in the 1990s. This, too, represents progress, but there is growing evidence that it has not gone far enough.

A theory that racism must be considered as a key component in any effort to understand depression in black Americans is emerging. The theory, advanced primarily by African American researchers and psychotherapists such as Dr. Sandra Walker in Seattle, Dr. Michelle Clark in San Francisco, Dr. Carl Bell in Chicago, and Dr. Alvin Poussaint in Boston, holds that the prevalence, severity, and treatment of depression in blacks are affected by questions ranging from the legacy of slavery to the racism that lingers in American society today.

Advocates of this theory don't argue that race explains everything regarding African Americans and depression and other mental disorders. They do maintain that there is clear evidence that race has an impact on the occurrence of mental illness and affects how best to treat it. Their goal is to generate discussion and research in the mental health community so that vital unanswered questions can be resolved.

Poussaint raised the issue in a lecture on minorities and mental health at the Carter Center in Atlanta in the fall of 2000. I spoke with Dr. Poussaint several times about these issues, including a long interview concerning *Lay My Burden Down,* his groundbreaking book on blacks and suicide. He clearly is as knowledgeable about these subjects as anyone on the planet. He is generous in sharing what he knows and what he believes to be true, yet he ended all our conversations with this cautionary mantra: "The data simply aren't there." To illustrate that point, Dr. Poussaint told me that he found the generally accepted statistics about suicide in America highly suspect in reflecting the rate at which black men end their own lives. The reasons for this, he believes, range from the strong stigma attached to suicide in the black community, so that people conceal it whenever possible, to the fact that some means of self-killing such as "suicide by cop"—in which people intentionally provoke police officers to shoot them—are not accepted as suicides by those who keep the records, even though this kind of action motivated by an obvious death wish is known in the black community as a method of suicide.

For Dr. Poussaint, the question remains, How can we expect to do something about the problem of suicide among African Americans when we know so little about the scope of the problem, especially among young black men, the group that clearly is at greatest risk of suicide? We are not guided by reliable information on how many African Americans kill themselves, much less why they do it and by what methods. The same kind of information deficit exists regarding depression and black men. We have not gathered enough information to determine the scope of the problem. Our society, in fact, has largely pretended that there is no problem. This is especially true in the black community. Our denial about depression might be called benign neglect if the effect of that neglect weren't so destructive and deadly. That makes it anything but benign.

Before I could understand the depth and danger of my own depression, I needed to break through my ignorance of the illness and my acceptance of stereotypes of what it means to be a black man. Overcoming these barriers took more than two decades. That delay almost cost me my life.

Bouts of depression have plagued me for as long as I can remember, even when I was a child. I could be moody. Smiles didn't seem to come as easily for me as they did for other children. I have a distinct memory of the first time I thought of suicide. I was nine or ten years old. I told my mother I wanted to go play baseball with some friends, and she said no. This was a minor thing, of course, but for some reason I felt devastated and bereft. Life didn't seem worth living. I remember thinking that I should find some high place and jump to my death. Obviously, I didn't do it. I was just a kid, after all, and like anyone that age I didn't hold on to thoughts for very long, not even thoughts of suicide. I probably remembered some comic book I hadn't finished and found a quiet place to read it. Life was worth living again.

But the depressions I fell into got longer and deeper as I got older. As I mentioned earlier, I believe now that my initial episode of serious depression struck when I left Georgia for my first full-time newspaper job in Detroit back in 1973. After my diagnosis of clinical depression, and as I learned more about the disease, I looked at my time in Detroit in retrospect, hoping to find the roots of my depression. Was there something about being so far away from home for the first time that tipped me toward my emotional downturn? Was I overwhelmed by working at one of the nation's largest newspapers fresh out of college? Was I unsuited for life in such a big city? There could have been a hundred other factors. Figuring out which ones mattered required me to examine my Detroit days in detail.

I remember moving to Detroit as an adventure. I had never been outside Georgia for more than a long weekend. Now I was living "up North" in a city that was a different world for me.

Detroit had a bad reputation. The "Motor City" had become "Murder City" as Detroit's murder rate was reported to be the worst in the nation. Its image was that of an ugly, crime-ridden, industrial wasteland. Almost everyone I told about my plans to leave Atlanta for Detroit thought I was crazy.

But I liked Detroit. It was an exotic place for someone who grew up in Jackson, Georgia. In Detroit, I had Chinese food for the first time in my life. Trips to downtown Detroit's Greektown exposed me to dishes I had never even heard of. In Atlanta, as in most Southern cities apart from New Orleans, the population was primarily divided into black and white. In Detroit, there were Italians, Poles, Irish, Hispanics, Greeks, and other groups in significant numbers, all united in their distinctiveness. Even the familiar took on new meaning for me in Detroit. In city hall, I came across a large map that identified neighborhoods by ethnicity. Among the identifiable groups was "Southern whites." I had never thought of plain ol' Southern white folks as belonging to an ethnic group.

My apartment was in one of the city's most notorious neighborhoods: the Cass Corridor, so called because of the major thoroughfare that ran through it. The sight of three or four police cars with blue lights flashing converging on a bar was a regular weekend occurrence. People in the *Free Press* newsroom actually laughed out loud when I told them where I lived. They thought it hilarious that the unsuspecting Southerner had been snookered into renting an apartment in "crime central."

Despite its dangers and drawbacks, my inner-city neighborhood had the three advantages that real estate agents always tout: Location. Location. Location. I was within walking distance of the *Free Press*'s downtown office building, Wayne State University (where I could catch art films for free), the main public library, and the city's art museum. Of course, "walking distance" is a relative term. I grew up a country boy who thought nothing of walking two or three miles or more to get somewhere. Hopping into a car seldom was an option, since my mother didn't drive and our family didn't own an automobile until I was a senior in high school anyway. I didn't have a car the first three months I lived in Detroit.

When I told colleagues about my walking tours of the city they again thought I was crazy, not just for footing it to so many places, but also for venturing into hazardous territory with no means of rapid escape. Yet I enjoyed my role as an urban explorer.

I also enjoyed my job at the newspaper, though my career as a reporter had a less than auspicious beginning. After a few days of rewriting press releases, I was given my first real assignment. I was sent to cover the dedication of a modern art sculpture in the middle of downtown. Lots of local dignitaries attended the event. I moved from one to another, gathering quotes for my article. Going through my routine with one man, I identified myself as a reporter for the *Free Press* and asked him what he thought of the artwork. Then I asked for his name. I asked his age. And, finally, asked him what he did for a living. The man looked at me with a tight smile and said, "Young man, I'm the publisher of your newspaper." At that point I began praying that I would still have a job at the end of the day.

I kept my job, and I became fairly good at it, too. When I did the cub reporter's usual stint as a night police reporter I managed to make the front of the metro section with a few stories that didn't rely on blood and gore to create reader interest. It wasn't long before I was in the *Free Press* City-County Bureau. I covered the County Commission, which was as dysfunctional as any governing body could be. All the reporters and political insiders joked and laughed about what a circus the commission was, but the reporting on it was straightforward and serious. As a newcomer taking a fresh look at what was going on, I had the radical idea of writing about the commission members as they really were, clown suits and all. So I wrote about the constant bickering and frequent personal insults the commissioners hurled at each other during their meetings.

That late summer and early fall in Detroit were a heady time. Yet even in the midst of my excitement over being in a new city and at the beginning of my chosen career, there were moments of unprovoked sadness. In those moments I was transmogrified from urban explorer to urban ghost. I haunted the places I went, instead of experiencing them. I was there, but I wasn't there. I roamed the city's streets like windblown paper. I felt empty.

These periods of melancholy were vague, ill defined at first. But as time passed, as the days shortened and the temperature dropped, the sorrow sharpened and began cutting into my soul.

Any number of things can trigger mild depression, from homesickness to the breakup of a relationship to a traumatic event such as the death of a loved one. Everyone responds to such events with some degree of sadness. For most people, the sadness is proportionate to the event that precipitated it, and it usually doesn't last inappropriately long. People have a way of bouncing back.

That is not how it works for those of us who suffer from clinical depression. Like everyone else, we may react to specific events by becoming sad. But our brains are different. The reason may be a chemical imbalance. Genetics may play a part. So may trauma, either physical or psychological. For whatever reason, our sadness can be not only more deeply felt, but also debilitating. We can be plunged into the depths by things that seem insignificant to other people. In fact, there are times when sadness seems to seize us out of the blue for no apparent reason. And we don't bounce back quickly.

Truth be told, I don't believe my major depression in Detroit was brought on by homesickness or any of the other usual precipitating events. I believe it was the weather. Many studies have shown that depression is affected by the seasons. In fact, the shortening of daylight hours with the onset of fall can lead to a form of depression called seasonal affective disorder (SAD). The most likely times for someone to be admitted to a hospital for treatment of depression are in the spring and autumn. (By the same token, suicides—which often involve depression—peak in the spring and summer.) This would suggest that the move from the sunny South to the long and bleak winters of Detroit would be a tonic for depression, not the cause of it.

But hospitalization for depression indicates that the illness has reached a serious stage. It can take some time to get to that point. Some researchers believe the start of those spring depressions would date back to the winter months. It has been demonstrated that our decreased exposure to light during winter's shorter days brings about physiological changes in the brain. As the seasons change, so do humans' bodies and minds. The changes wrought by winter give a lot of people the blues—aka "cabin fever." Again, most people bounce back. People who suffer from clinical or severe depression don't.

I believe that explains what happened to me when I moved to Detroit. Arriving there at the end of the summer of 1973, I was amazed at how quickly fall fled and winter blew in and took over. The stretches of cold and cloudy days seemed endless. I had never gone so long without seeing the sun in my life. After one particularly long period of slate-gray skies was broken by a sunny day, the *Free Press* ran a tongue-in-cheek editorial informing readers that the bright object that had appeared overhead the previous day was called the sun.

Soon, I was weighed down by a major depression that was obvious to everyone around me. I wasn't isolated in Detroit—I made life-long friends at the newspaper, and they tried to help me. One friend in particular decided the way to cheer me up was to introduce me to Detroit's topless bars. It didn't work. We'd step out of the warmth of wine and women and there would be Detroit's dreary winter waiting for us.

When I think now about the documented scientific evidence of how seasonal changes can affect the mind adversely and about my own negative reaction to the climatic changes that came with my move from Georgia to Detroit, I wonder about the slaves who were brought to this country. What was it like for those snatched from tropical areas and transplanted to temperate zones of the United States? Even in the Deep South, there were seasonal changes the Africans had never experienced. Was this alone enough to cause depression in some of them? I would venture a guess that it did.

During my episode of depression in Detroit—what I now look

back on as the winter solstice of my soul—no one suggested that I get professional help. Nor did the idea occur to me. I had never heard of anyone seeking medical treatment because they were unhappy. In any event, even though my depression couldn't have been more apparent had I worn a flashing neon sign that read, "I am depressed," I couldn't bring myself to actually tell anyone how I was feeling.

I certainly had opportunities to do so. I realize now that two of my best friends at the *Free Press* were themselves fighting through bouts of depression. One in particular was having a tough time of it. I walked into the office one morning and found him pressed up against a window. He was staring intently at the street twelve stories below.

"What's up?" I asked. "Whatcha doin'?"

He didn't turn away from the window. "I was just thinking how much better things would be if I could open this window and jump out," he said. His voice was flat, and he wasn't smiling.

I didn't know what to say beyond the usual "Things can't be that bad." I didn't understand that things really *could* be that bad. I had no inkling that someday things would be that bad for me. Although I was in the throes of my first major depression, I was not yet suicidal. I had neither a frame of reference nor the words to talk about what my friend was going through and what I was destined to go through myself in a few years. Even if I had had the words back then, I doubt I would have spoken them.

My Detroit friend eventually found his way back from the dark place in which I found him that morning. He rediscovered personal joy and professional success. To this day, he is happy and prosperous. I eventually learned that he got treatment for his depression. I wish I could have helped him as a friend. But, back then, I couldn't even help myself. There had been nothing in my life experiences to prepare me to fight that battle.

The black men who were my role models when I was growing up bore whatever hardship life handed them with quiet dignity. They didn't complain. They didn't even talk about their troubles. Church was the only place I ever saw anything resembling an outpouring of emotion by these men. When they were "shouting" or "had the Holy Ghost," they might perform a kind of stomping dance and flail about so violently that church ushers had to restrain them to keep them from hurting themselves or other congregants. But the most striking thing to me was to see the emotional outbursts that erupted from these stoic men. They would cry out, often detailing the miseries they had suffered and thanking God for allowing them to hold up under this burden. The men often had tears streaming down their faces. This is a deeply spiritual experience, but I believe it also is psychologically therapeutic, allowing black men to release pent-up emotions in a culturally acceptable way. But I knew even as a child that outside the church any display involving the shedding of tears would be considered unmanly.

So these men kept their emotions under control and to themselves. That was one of the reasons they were admired in the community. They stood in contrast to the men whose emotions *were* on public display. Those were the men who let loose their anger, sometimes acting it out in violence. They were the men I was warned against emulating. Someone who kept his emotions restrained— except in church—was the type of man I was told I should grow up to be.

Keep quiet and snap out of it. That's what I told myself when my depression was at its worst. Eventually, I did snap out of it. The bounceback coincided with my decision to leave Detroit and return to Atlanta, where I had a standing job offer at the *Atlanta Journal,* I thought then that I had had a bad case of the blues and that moving back South had cured it. I was wrong. I had no idea I was dealing with an illness that is as much a part of me as chronic heart disease is a part of someone living with that ailment. And I didn't have a clue about how dangerous my illness was.

I hope what once was said of former president Gerald Ford when he first ran for Congress can be said of me and my lack of understanding of clinical depression: "He's not dumb. He's just ignorant." I had no idea I needed to get information essential to understanding depression. Even when I was in my forties, my idea of depression didn't go much beyond a vague notion that it was a state of sadness that went on for a long time. I had no sense of the clinical meaning of the term, no concept of it as an illness of the mind that could be treated. This might seem remarkable for someone who spent more than twenty years as a journalist, inundated with information about everything under the sun, but it really isn't, given the attitudes toward depression generally held by the public and particularly held by the African American community.

Through ignorance, I failed to understand the classic symptoms of clinical depression as I experienced them in Detroit and for years afterward. I endured the bouts of sadness that stretched into weeks and months, the lack of interest in things that usually gave me pleasure, the disruptions in my sleep patterns (I was either unable to sleep, or would spend most of my nonworking hours asleep), the lack of energy, the irritability, the confused thinking that made decision-making difficult, the emotional frailty, and the feeling of hopelessness that made me believe things would never get better.

My view of what it meant to be black in America—and especially of what it meant to be a black man in America—allowed me to ignore some symptoms as nothing more than my expected lot in life. It also left me too embarrassed to acknowledge my other emotional difficulties, let alone talk to other people about them. My acculturation taught me that sadness and a sense of hopelessness go with being African American, and so did having the inner strength to overcome those feelings. As I said before, it also taught me that being a man meant keeping emotions under control and, even more important, never, ever showing them.

Depression, I found, has a devious way of disrupting someone's emotional life. It made me more emotional while at the same time it diminished my ability to deal with my emotions. Depression convinced me that everything in my life was a path toward one destination. That destination was unhappiness. I believed nothing in the world could prevent me from reaching that unpleasant place. Even love, when viewed through depression's distorted lens, was no source of happiness. This view of life took hold of me even before the illness reached its most serious phase. My depression was at a middle stage, like a constant low-grade fever that I could live with as long as I was willing to suffer its symptoms.

I did finally reach the point that I decided to get professional help, if only to stop the people around me from telling me that that was what I should do. The decision came in 1996, more than twenty years after my first encounter with severe depression in Detroit. I made up my mind after coming close to making a suicide attempt. I saw Dr. June Serravezza, a psychiatrist whose name was on a referral list of psychotherapists provided by my wife's employee assistance program. Dr. Serravezza's office was the closest to home. For me, that was reason enough to select her. I gave no thought to what qualities a therapist should have to meet my needs: I didn't take the idea of getting help all that seriously.

So I walked into Dr. Serravezza's office a skeptic. I was still one when I walked out of her office that first time. I didn't really reveal much of myself to her that day. I talked as little as possible about my emotional problems and concentrated on the physical symptoms of my depression, mainly my lack of sleep.

Still, my state of denial, my less-than-blissful ignorance about what depression meant, gradually had begun falling away, even before my first visit to Dr. Serravezza. The sign I couldn't ignore was my inability to control my emotions. I remember my reaction to the O. J. Simpson verdict on October 3, 1995, in particular. I followed the case closely, with what I thought was a journalist's analytical objectivity. I weighed the evidence carefully and decided that the scales tipped heavily toward Simpson's guilt.

Members of the *Constitution* editorial board gathered in a conference room to watch the jury come back after its surprisingly short deliberations. When the court clerk read the words "Not guilty," the reaction in that conference room was stunned silence. I did manage to whisper, "Wow, he got away with it," but that was about all.

I went back to my cubicle, trying to understand the jurors' reasoning. Was it the prosecution's general ineptitude, with the try-on-the-bloody-glove fiasco being the prime example? Did the lies and racism of LAPD detective Mark Fuhrman make a police conspiracy seem not just believable, but likely? Could the evidence that meant one thing to me mean something entirely different to someone else?

So there I sat, Mr. On-the-One-Hand-On-the-Other-Hand, and before I knew what was happening tears were running down my face. I wasn't on either side of the emotional divide that had opened across the country only moments earlier, when it seemed everyone was either jumping for joy that O.J. had beaten the rap or hopping mad that he had gotten away with murder. I felt neither joy nor anger. I felt a deep and abiding sadness. I could not get images of Nicole Brown Simpson and Ron Goldman out of my mind. I imagined their fear and suffering during the slaughter. I pictured a man butchering the mother of his children. The tears flowed. I couldn't stop them. I could only pray that no one saw me.

That episode foreshadowed the day a few months later when the house of cards built from my rationalizations about my depression would finally collapse. The fall came with what to me was a thunderous crash. I was at work, standing at a fifth-floor window, observing the comings and goings of people below on that bright and beautiful day. It was early in 1996, and Atlanta already was electric with anticipation of the Centennial Summer Olympics, which the city was to host. I watched the lunchtime crowd. There were couples walking together. Groups of people stood at street corners, laughing and talking. I looked down at these signs of human happiness and was filled with an unfathomable sadness. Everything I saw seemed to defy the disconnectedness and loneliness I felt. A wall of my own making surrounded me, separating me from family and friends. I had fought for months to keep people at a distance. My greatest fear was that I had succeeded all too well.

Suddenly, something deep inside me began to break loose and well up. Tears ran down my face and my chest heaved with uncontrollable sobs. It felt as if I was swimming in sorrow. Actually, it was more like being submerged in sorrow. Great gulps of sadness filled my lungs. The more I took in, the more I suffocated. I was panicked and mortified. My unemotional façade had fallen away.

At that moment, the effect of depression that I feared most descended upon me. I could tolerate almost all of the symptoms; I could even rationalize them as admirable character traits. If I refused to communicate, I was the strong, silent type. If I isolated myself from others, I was a self-sufficient lone wolf. If I found no pleasures in life, I was purifying myself by choosing the path of monastic self-sacrifice. It's actually easy to find such enticements in depression once you decide the disease is part of who you are. But I could not rationalize, I could find nothing to admire about myself, as depression descended on me and I broke down into tears in that fifth-floor office.

My manhood was unraveling for the world to see. Everything I believed made me a man was being stripped away. I can't remember much of what I was thinking as this happened; I was feeling more than thinking, in fact. I felt something being cut from the core of me, as if I were undergoing a castration of male emotional control. I wasn't getting in touch with my feminine side. I was being pushed unwillingly into the realm of hyperfemininity.

From the time in our boyhoods when we are old enough to understand, black males are taught to value manhood. Manhood is so prized that, all too often, some settle for the most superficial imitations of it. When we measure our manhood in sexual conquests, atheletic prowess, brutality, easy money, and all the other glittering counterfeits of masculinity, we hold something less valuable than fool's gold. That gives us all the more reason to hold on to the real thing when we believe we have it. But as my emotional crisis deepened, I felt the calm stoicism I associated with manhood draining from me.

I didn't want to behave this way, and, more than anything, I didn't want anyone to see me this way. But someone did. One of my supervisors, a woman named Susan Stevenson, was walking by. She stopped. Susan is a fair but tough, no-nonsense manager. She especially doesn't like listening to people whine instead of doing what it takes to solve a problem and get the job done. I could only imagine what she thought of me, this person she knew as quiet and unemotional, someone for whom a smile was a grudging giveaway of what he was feeling. Yet there I stood, the floodgates fully open and my face twisted into a mask of anguish.

"What's wrong?" she asked.

I doubt I said anything intelligible through my sobbing. I was trying to say something I had been feeling for a long time, but which I had never said to anyone: "I can't take this anymore."

And, at that moment, I really *couldn't* take it anymore. I felt desperation, hopelessness, and pain. I just wanted it all to end. Had there been some way to open the fifth-floor window I might have climbed through and jumped. Fortunately, my coworkers were away from their desks for lunch. The office was pretty much empty. But they would be coming back soon, and I had no hope of getting myself under control by then. What was happening was worse than a nightmare, because not even in a dream world gone completely wrong could I have imagined behaving the way I was behaving at that moment.

Susan stepped forward and put her arms around me. She pulled me close and murmured, "Don't worry. It'll be all right."

I did not—I could not—believe that. But at that moment, those words and the caring way in which they were said were exactly what I needed.

Susan had the presence of mind to ask whether I was seeing a doctor. I pulled Dr. Serravezza's card from my wallet and handed it to her. She called the number and explained what had happened. Then she put me on the phone.

Dr. Serravezza said she thought I was having an anxiety attack. "Do you feel like you're calming down?" she asked. "As time goes by, are you feeling better or worse?"

"I'm calming down," I said, though I'm sure I didn't sound that way. The crying had not stopped, and I still struggled to get words out. "I think I'm feeling better."

"Well, I want you to get out of there and just walk around for a little if you feel up to it," she said. "I think that'll help. I'm going to call in a prescription for some Klonopin. That's an anti-anxiety medication. I want you to pick that up and take some right away. Do you think you can do that on your own, or do you need to call someone to come pick you up?"

"I can do it."

"Okay. You do that. Then I want to get you in here this afternoon, as soon as you can."

I was calming down. I *was* feeling better. Even so, there remained a sense of unreality about what was happening to me. Not that I imagined that the things transpiring in that office weren't truly taking place. Rather, I felt I was outside of what was happening, at a vantage point from which I could look down at myself. Depression often is described as an enveloping darkness, an image that harks back to the concept of the body flooded with dark humors. But there is an electric brightness about depression mixed with anxiety. The world seems illuminated by an arc light. Everything is all too starkly visible. That's how the scene in which I was both spectacle and witness was lighted.

What I saw filled me with a fear brewed from horror and hopelessness. For a few moments I was afraid as I had never been afraid before. I was not afraid of anything I could name. I was afraid of *everything*—afraid of life, afraid of the existence of the world. The fear was painful. It doubled back on me and made me afraid that it would be with me forever.

The moment I left the newspaper building that day, I started to dread going back. How could I face people at work again? Hardly anyone had seen what happened; but I felt a cruel certainty that by the end of the day there would hardly be anyone who didn't know that something shameful had happened to me. I averted my gaze from anyone I encountered as I fled the scene of my "crime." I wanted no one to see my reddened eyes or the tears that still brimmed there. These were the evidence of my weakness. They had to be hidden from the world.

Dr. Sandra Walker, an African American psychoanalyst who practices in Seattle, came to Atlanta in the spring of 2000 to talk about race and mental health. During her visit she screened and led a discussion of the movie *Sankofa* at Emory University. The film, by the Ethiopian-born filmmaker Haile Gerima, is an intense examination of slavery—from capture in Africa to captivity in America. Most of those attending were students at the university, and most were majoring in psychology or studying psychiatry at the medical school. This audience should have been receptive to Dr. Walker's message that it is therapeutic for blacks and whites to confront slavery and its lingering legacy.

But when the film ended, a young white man immediately left his seat to confront Dr. Walker. "How can showing something like this help bring about racial reconciliation?" he demanded. "It shows white people only as cruel and evil!"

Dr. Walker tried to explain that the movie, made by an African filmmaker, told the story of slavery from a black perspective. The whites in the film were slave traders and slave owners. So, yes, those people were portrayed as cruel and evil.

The man would have none of it. He said discussing the film was worse than useless, then stormed out of the auditorium.

This exchange exemplifies an attitude toward slavery held by many whites. They are tired of having blacks throw slavery in their faces and holding them responsible for the sins of their ancestors. Couple that attitude with skepticism about depression as an illness, and it's clear that making a connection between slavery and depression among African Americans is a tough sell. When Dr. Alvin Poussaint talks about "post-traumatic slavery syndrome," much of America will refuse to listen.

In fact, it is clear that there isn't enough general interest in this country in finding answers to some very basic questions about African Americans, especially about black men. It's as if there is no reason to suspect that depression is any different for black men than it is for other Americans. But there are differences, differences that affect how depression may be triggered in African American men, how it may manifest itself in us, and what treatments are most effective for us.

Dr. Michelle Clark is a San Francisco psychiatrist and founder of the University of San Francisco's Black Focus Program, which researches and structures treatments that meet the special needs of black mental health patients. She believes that racism affects the mental health of African Americans just as it affects other aspects of our lives. Dr. Clark says African American men face a double whammy when it comes to depression: Being men, we're less likely to acknowledge and do something about the illness; being black in America, we are subjected to additional stresses that can lead to depression.

I spoke also with Dr. Carl Bell about this. He's president and chief executive officer of the Community Mental Health Council in Chicago and a professor of psychiatry at the University of Illinois. He cited one example of something that may happen to black Americans every day and can have a negative impact on our mental health. He calls it the "micro insult."

For a black person, a micro insult is the miniature cousin of an overtly racist comment, Dr. Bell explained. It may not register on anyone's radar screen. The person who issues the insult is probably unaware of having done it. The person who is insulted may not consciously recognize that he or she has been insulted. They may have a nagging feeling that they've suffered some harm, even if they can't identify the source of the hurt. Dr. Bell supplied this example from his own experience:

"I had an appointment with a doctor I was seeing for the first time. I went up to the receptionist to sign in. She asked me for my Medicaid card. I told her I didn't have Medicaid; I had private health insurance. That was that.

"But something was bothering me. Why did she automatically think I was on Medicaid? It could only be because I'm black. I'm sure that woman didn't realize she had said anything remotely racist. Yet, in my mind, what she said was a racist insult. Imagine how things like that can pile up. It has to take a toll."

There is a dearth of data on the toll taken by the piling up of these tiny, racially tinged psychological traumas. There is plenty of anecdotal evidence, some of it as plain as the look on the faces of many African American men. One of the things June Serravezza said to me at the end of my first session in her office was that I looked depressed. I had never realized that the misery I thought I was hiding in my heart was displayed on my face. I did have a brooding, somber countenance most of the time. I had the look of an unhappy man.

Dr. Serravezza's comment made me think of "the look." It's an expression people see on the faces of so many young black men on the street, on the subway or anywhere else. People see "the look" and they see a young man who is "mad and bad." They see someone who looks dangerous and should be avoided at all costs. They cross over to the other side of the street. They move to the other end of the subway car.

But I believe that for many of these men the look isn't just about being mad and bad. It's the outward manifestation of what they feel inside, feelings rooted in unhappiness and hopelessness. For many black men, "the look" is the look of depression.

Such subtleties make up the "micro" side of the impact of racism on mental health. There's also a "macro" side, and it's a huge historical and lingering stress in the lives of African Americans. This is the kind of incident in which there is nothing subtle about the racism involved; the insult, the discrimination, the oppression—whatever it may be—is overt and beyond misinterpretation. That's how it fulfills its role in the system that perpetuates racial inequality.

Almost all African Americans have experienced such incidents; they are imprinted in our memories. This is especially true of those of us who came of age before the benefits of the civil rights movement became widespread. For me, the memories play back like scenes from a vivid film. Among my mental movies:

My first close encounter with white people. *I was of preschool age. My older sister and I were making the short walk from our house to an* aunt's house. Three little white girls were playing in the front yard of one of the houses we had to walk past. Seeing us coming, the girls ran to the edge of the yard, almost onto the sidewalk. I heard their sweet, singsong voices as we got closer. I couldn't make out what they were singing at first. I expected a childhood ditty like any of those I might sing while at play. As the words became clear, however, this is what I heard the little girls singing: "Black niiiigers. Black niiiigers. Black nii-iigers . . ." "Don't pay no attention," my sister said, but the "angelic" voices followed us until we were out of earshot.

My first, brief conversation with a white adult. *I was in the first or second grade. Walking home from school one day, I saw a white man and his dog coming toward me. The man looked old but not elderly. His dog was small, but I could tell it was full grown. It had nothing of puppy playfulness about it. It began growling as it got close to me. That stopped me and rooted my feet to the ground. The dog began sniffing me, keeping up its growl.*

"You scared of him?" the man asked.

"Yes, sir," I said.

"Don't worry," the man said, looking down at me with a smile. "He's just smelling you to see if you're a nigger."

My realization that lynching happened in my world. *I was in elementary school, perhaps in the sixth or seventh grade. I heard that an older brother of one of my classmates disappeared after being released from jail. His body was found on a country back road. Someone had repeatedly run over him with a car. This was not something that had happened over in Mississippi, and about which I was reading in* Jet *magazine. This happened in my hometown; it happened to a family I knew. Word of it quickly spread through the black community. My friend's brother had been involved with a white girl, and the secret got out. Local Klansmen killed him, and a white merchant was widely rumored to have been the ringleader. No one was arrested for the crime. People in the black community talked about getting something done, but nothing ever came of it. I saw how little power the grown-ups around me really had, and, somewhere in the recesses of my subconscious, I must have drawn the conclusion that I had no power at all.*

I see that the people who hate me are confident that they will prevail. *The day after Dr. Martin Luther King, Jr., was assassinated in Memphis, the killing was the only topic being discussed at school. His death was devastating for the dozen or so of us black students attending the formerly all-white high school under the "freedom of choice" school desegregation plan. But there was jubilation among many of the more than three hundred white students at Jackson High. They walked the halls smiling, if not laughing out loud. One of my classmates made this joke: "They said the suspect was a well-dressed white man. If they catch him, he'll be charged with hunting coons out of season." Clearly, the white students thought everything had changed with this one act of murder. (They must have seen confirmation of it when black students boycotted classes one day the following week in protest of the assassination. Their school was all-white once again, if only for a few hours.) What the episode showed me was how the whites around me saw the struggle for racial equality as marginal and temporary. Get rid of the chief troublemaker, they thought, and blacks will get back in their place. It's frightening to know that people who have an interest in your oppression believe this and have the power to act on it.*

I've often heard it argued that as times change and racism recedes, the hurt it caused us should be relegated to the past. We should move on and not dwell on things that can't be undone. But even when we move on, we have to understand how our history shapes who we are. We may move beyond the routine emotional traumas of adolescence yet still feel their effects on a subconscious level. This also is true of the emotional traumas resulting from racism.

How resistant is white America to the idea that blacks suffer emotional harm as a result of racism? Consider how the courts generally handle the issue. Our legal system accepts the concept that a complainant should be compensated by someone who causes him to suffer "extreme emotional distress." But cases based on the claim that blacks suffer emotional distress because of racism have been greeted with judicial skepticism, often because courts minimize African Americans' interpretation of the meaning and impact of racist words and symbols. There was a Georgia case, for example, in which black workers for a utility company sought damages for the emotional pain they suffered as result of their white coworkers' racism. Among other things, nooses were placed in black workers' lockers, and racist jokes were frequently told in the workplace. The case was thrown out in March 2003 by a federal judge who ruled that while a victim of racial discrimination can file suit for financial damages, someone who is exposed to racism per se can't seek compensation. The judge went on to say, in effect, that racism is so ingrained in American society that blacks ought to be used to it. It's as if our exposure to racism has vaccinated us against the mental anguish of racial oppression.

Unfortunately, there is no such immunity. How could bigotry of any kind not leave lingering emotional scars on its victims? Dr. Martin Luther King, Jr., said racism instilled in black Americans a "degenerating sense of nobody-ness." That's a pretty good description of depression.

In 1986 I cowrote a magazine article about the twentieth anniversary of freedom-of-choice desegregation of schools in my hometown. Four black students attended the "white" school in the first year of the plan. When I tracked down the three surviving students and interviewed them for the article, I was struck by how their emotional reactions to what happened to them two decades before remained fresh. One former student told me a story from that time in a voice so pained he could have been recounting an incident from the day before.

In the midst of the abuse he suffered in that first year, he met one white student with whom he developed a friendship. This student would actually talk to him. They began hanging out together after school sometimes. This, the black student had thought, was why what he went through to integrate the school was worthwhile: Black students and white students would see each other as people and learn that they could get along.

One day, the white student suggested that they stop by a downtown restaurant for a hamburger on the way home from school.

"We went in and sat down at a table," the man told me those twenty years later. "A man came out and said, 'He can't eat in here. He has to go around the side.' On the side of the restaurant they had this little room where black people went. There was a window into the kitchen where you could order something to take out. The man was telling me again that I had to leave. People in the restaurant were looking. I got up to go, and I thought my friend would leave with me. But he didn't. He just sat there. He stayed and had his food while I had go. That hurt me worse than anything else that happened that year. I thought he was my friend, and he wasn't.

"Things like that made me hate white people," he said. "I hated them then and I hate them now. I don't want to hate anyone, but the things we went through that year showed me what white people are really like."

Racial hatred isn't considered a mental disorder—though Dr. Alvin Poussaint and others have campaigned to have extreme racism included among diagnosable mental disorders—but it was clear that what that man was feeling twenty years after the fact caused him emotional distress. He reacted to racism with racism, a belief system he knew was fundamentally wrong and one he didn't want to guide him. What are the aftereffects of racism that others feel, perhaps for decades? Anxiety? Depression? Many people suffer the wounds of racism and seem none the worse for it. Yet it seems inescapable that being a target of racism—living a life in which your ability to control your own destiny is diminished and in which you are constantly vulnerable to violence and abuse—would put you at high risk for psychological damage.

To understand the risk of emotional trauma, you have to understand something about what happened to the United States on September 11, 2001.

When hijackers flew two passenger jets into the twin towers of the World Trade Center and another into the Pentagon, while a fourth plane was forced to crash by passengers before it reached its target, international terrorism on the largest scale ever came to America's shores. We realized that we are not out of the reach of groups around

the world who hate our nation. Americans learned that we have enemies who are beyond our control, who either believe that they will
not be punished by us or who hate us so much that no punishment
will deter their violence toward us.

This feeling of vulnerability had all sorts of impacts on this country. There are indications that one impact was an increase in the
occurrence of depression among Americans. Mental health clinics
reported increases in the number of people who came in seeking
treatment for depression. There were increases in the number of prescriptions for antidepressants. And these things didn't manifest
themselves only in New York City, and Washington, D.C., and
Pennsylvania, where the acts of terrorism took place. They happened
across the country.

Speaking about the September 11 attacks at a 2002 symposium
sponsored by the Carter Center's Mental Health Program, Dr.
Robert Ursano said, "Our mental health is the target of terrorist
events." Ursano, director of the Center for the Study of Traumatic
Stress, added, "Terrorism tries to undermine our sense of morale,
our cohesion, our ability to look to the future with hope and to sustain our communities and our families."

The victims of the attacks aren't the only ones who feel threatened
by acts of terrorism, he said. Those who identify with the victims,
whether as residents of the same community, members of the same
ethnic group, or citizens of the same nation, fear being potential targets of the terror. They also share in the emotional harm done by the
terrorist acts. "We know that the greater the threat, the higher the
number of psychiatric disorders we will see," Ursano said. "That has
been found in every study that has ever been done."

It should have come as no surprise, then, that many Americans'
mental health was adversely affected by the unprecedented threat
that invaded our lives on September 11, 2001. It was reasonable that
many people reacted to the attacks with anxiety, pessimism, and a
feeling that they had lost some control of their own fates. It was even
reasonable that some people felt hopeless. Most people were able to
move beyond such feelings fairly quickly. But for some of the many

who were prone to depression, the terrorism probably triggered the illness.

Now consider the conditions in which many African Americans have lived for much of our history in this country. Our fate has been in the hands of people who thought of us as less than human or who even hated us outright. They could punish us on a whim and could attack us with little or no fear of retribution. Since slavery ended we've been subject to intimidation and murder by night riders, church bombers, and rogue racists. These people were terrorists, in essence, and many African Americans lived in fear of becoming victims of terrorism.

We've witnessed the effect one day of terrorism had on the mental health of Americans. Now imagine people spending their entire lives under the threat of terrorism—for generation after generation. What would be the impact on their mental health? Consider that black men were the chief targets of this racial terrorism because they were more feared and because the patriarchal nature of the civil rights movement made men the most visible—and thus the most hated—activists. Also, consider that even today black men know that they are statistically the most likely among Americans to become victims of fatal violence and that even law-abiding African American men may tense up at the sight of a police officer. Given these conditions, the question is hardly whether there's a problem with depression among black men. When the few studies that attempt to sort out the prevalence of depression in black men report rates roughly the same as those among white men, the question becomes, How on earth can the rate for black men *not* be higher?

What I feel in my gut and what I've learned in researching this book tell me that there is a serious problem with depression among African American men. That makes sense because of the conditions in which we, as black men, live. But, as Alvin Poussaint says, no one has bothered to perform in-depth studies—not enough, at least, to say with confidence what the situation is. I also believe this country's troubled history of race, and its lingering racism, prevent Americans from accepting depression's destructive impact on black men and from confronting the problem.

Doctors and scientists—such as the teams led by Dr. DiAnne Bradford at Atlanta's Morehouse College School of Medicine and Dr. Michelle Clark at the University of California at San Francisco—are doing pioneering research into the racial dimensions of depression and its treatment. Activists such as Dr. Carl Bell in Chicago are advocating that more resources be devoted to dealing with depression and other mental illnesses among minorities. The researchers must continue their work. The activists must be heard. They are on paths toward acknowledging the true toll of depression on African American men, and toward understanding how to stop it.

THREE

When Racism and Depression Mix

I got the blues from my head to my shoes . . .
I've got a mean low down feelin'
I'm gonna hear bad news.

—Joe Oliver and Clarence Williams,
"West End Blues"

There's a scene in the movie *Casablanca* in which a young woman desperate to escape the Nazis asks Rick, the American café owner, what kind of man Louis Renault, the prefect of police, is. Rick answers, "He's a man like any other, only more so."

Depression in black men is like depression in other men, only more so. This is true because of the way racism can plunge African American men into depression and anchor them in the depth of the disease.

Researchers continue to add to our knowledge of the possible causes of clinical depression. A chemical imbalance in the brain appears to be to blame in many cases. There is evidence that genetics can play a role, but there is debate about how much of a role. Is clinical depression purely a genetic illness, in place at birth? Is it the result of a defect of the brain that develops over time and renders someone unable to cope with "precipitating events" such as the death of a loved one? Or is it a combination of nature and nurture:

an inherited predisposition to slip into deep depression after precipitating events?

As in many areas of scientific inquiry, however, the debate over the causes of depression shows that the more we know the less sure we are that we really understand. The theory that a chemical imbalance in the brain causes major depression has been researched for more than thirty years. At times there seemed confirmation enough for some to accept the theory as a scientific certainty. But the idea that this "biologic abnormality" is a cause of depression doesn't stand up so well when basic standards of scientific proof are applied. Those standards are laid out in the Surgeon General's Report on Mental Health:

> In the search for biological changes with depression, it must be understood that *a biological abnormality* reliably associated with depression may not actually be a causal factor. For example, a biologic alteration could be a consequence of sleep deprivation or weight loss. *Any biological abnormality* found in conjunction with any mental disorder might be a cause, a correlate, or a consequence. . . . What drives research is the determination to find which of *the biological abnormalities* in depression are true causes, especially ones that might be detectable and treatable *before* the onset of clinical symptoms.

In other words, it may be true that people who suffer major depression have an imbalance of certain chemicals in the brain, but that may not explain why this very complex illness struck them. It may be that we've found an explanation for a symptom of the disease, but not the cause of the disease itself. It would be as if a researcher determined that many people who suffer from the flu have an excess of mucus in their nasal passages and then claimed that this excess mucus was the cause of the flu. The excess mucus certainly is a factor in the effect of the illness; a runny nose makes it difficult for the sufferer to breathe. But it is not the cause.

Staying with the runny-nose analogy, it is easy to see why one of the "proofs" cited in favor of the chemical-imbalance theory has been undercut. As evidence of the chemical connection with depression, some researchers point to drugs that cause depression, and to antidepressant medications that apparently work by adjusting the chemical imbalance in the brain. However, that is like arguing that because decongestants work—they clear those stuffy nasal passages and make flu sufferers feel better—runny noses cause the flu.

Finally, there is the question whether the chemical imbalance theory meets the standard of scientific proof that would give it the greatest value for medical application: Does it provide a reliable way to identify those who suffer from depression *before* they exhibit symptoms of the disease? For some researchers, the answer is the same as it is for the runny nose: If you identify people who need treatment for the flu by looking for anyone with a runny nose, you're too late. Those people are already sick; the runny nose is just one of the symptoms.

"Depression can be the outcome of severe and prolonged stress," the Surgeon General's report says. Increasingly, research points to stress and other external factors as more than "triggering events" that set off episodes of major depression in people who are predisposed to suffer from the illness. Rather, it is apparent that such events can actually create the predisposition by influencing how the brain works, even changing the structure of the brain itself. For example, those brain chemicals may get out of balance in reaction to stress. Just as adrenaline is pumped into the bloodstream when we confront a situation requiring physical exertion, certain chemicals may be produced in the brain to help us cope with stress. But we may have evolved—and our environment may have changed—to the point that either we don't need the dose we once got, or the doses have become virtually constant and therefore too much for our systems to handle. In any case, where stress once may have generated an appropriate response, it now throws things out of whack.

And it's not just a matter of stress affecting the production of chemicals in the brain. "Interestingly, one new line of research finds that long-term consequences of anxiety and depression are evident at the same anatomical site—the hippocampus," the Surgeon General's report says. "Human imaging studies of the hippocampus revealed it to have smaller volume in patients with post-traumatic stress disorder and in patients with recurrent depression. In [one] study, the degree of volume reduction was correlated with the duration of major depression."

Some researchers theorize that depression isn't caused by abnormalities that make the brain go awry. Believing that the key isn't the process that produces our thoughts, but the thoughts themselves, they argue that we can cure depression by changing our cognitive patterns—what we think about things. The theory is based on the phenomenon called learned helplessness, which has been observed in experiments on laboratory animals. The animals were placed in an enclosure and subjected to electrical shocks. They could not run and they could not hide. No matter what they did, there was no way to avoid the shocks. The animals became resigned to the torture. They no longer tried to escape. They learned to be helpless. What was interesting was that when their environment changed, their helplessness didn't. They were placed in areas where there were obvious opportunities to avoid the shocks. Yet, the animals did nothing to escape the punishment. They simply took it.

By the same token, the theory holds, people suffering from depression have learned to be helpless. They think of the things that have happened to them and around them in the most negative light. Their behavior then follows their thought patterns. It isn't that simple, of course. The people who promote the idea that cognitive factors are important in understanding depression do allow that what we think may be influenced by our experiences and the way our brains work. But they still maintain that it's the thoughts that count, and if we can change those thoughts we can change everything.

In one respect, the debate about what really causes depression is beside the point. What's most important is finding a treatment that effectively provides relief for people suffering from the illness. It has been proven that correcting a chemical imbalance in the brain relieves symptoms of depression. For the people who suffer, finding a medication that works is all that matters.

But if we're interested in knowing which people are susceptible to clinical depression and how to protect them from developing the disease, we have to understand the causes. If those who argue for the importance of environmental factors and other nonbiologic causes of depression are correct, their ideas are especially important to understanding depression in African American men. The world we live in as black men is rife with conditions that are conducive to depression, according to theories that cite the importance of— among other things—stress, lack of control of one's own destiny, and negative thinking.

Dr. Alvin Poussaint's concept of post-traumatic slavery syndrome is compatible with all the current theories of depression's causes. Poussaint argues that the effects of slavery and racism are "in the blood" of African Americans, passed down from generation to generation. This may be the genetic brain characteristic that results in depression even in the absence of precipitating events, or it may be the predisposition to be affected by those events. This idea would not apply to African Americans only, of course: Every ethnic group has some trauma in its history. The ability to cope with the trauma may be handed down from generation to generation, but so may the vulnerability to that trauma's legacy. The passage of time isn't enough to heal the emotional damage inflicted on the group, especially if the source of the hurt persists, as racism persists in America.

As I noted in the previous chapter, I believe the role racism can play in the cause and course of clinical depression makes the disorder's impact on African American men more devastating. Throughout the history of black people in America, African American men have been targeted for racial discrimination and oppression more frequently and more vigorously. We are the ones who must be kept under control and in our place. From the days when Southern whites found themselves outnumbered by slaves, the greatest fear has been that black men might get out of control and refuse to stay in our "place."

Racism not only brings on depression in black men, it exacerbates the effects of the illness. For example, according to a study by the Centers for Disease Control and Prevention, blacks who suffer from depression are 160 percent more likely to have a stroke than other people. White men with depression were 68 percent more likely than others to have a stroke, while the risk of stroke for depressed white women was 52 percent higher. (The study differentiated between white men and white women, but lumped black men and black women together. If the gender gap between African American men and women is the same as that between white men and white women, it means black men with depression are 182 percent more likely to have a stroke than is the U.S. population as a whole.)

Most damaging and deadly for African American men, racism intensifies the sense of hopelessness that descends upon us when depression hits. To face racism is to struggle to maintain hope. Depression forces us to abandon hope. That's devastating for black men living in the environment to which poverty and racism have relegated them. Irritability escalates to violence. Fragile family ties are broken—why struggle to provide for your children when something deep inside you says there's no hope of the world becoming a better place for you, or for them?

*   *   *

Some of the views held by Dr. Alvin Poussaint, Dr. Michelle Clark, and others on racism's role in depression are controversial. They are subjects for debate among psychotherapists and researchers. Long-standing research shows that the stresses some groups face in their everyday lives do make the members of those groups more likely to suffer from mental disorders such as depression. I'll discuss that research more fully later. What I'll say here is that while those studies have not focused on race, their results provide ammunition for those who argue that racism has an impact on mental health.

In any case, it should be beyond debate that racism is a factor in African American men's lack of access to mental health care. This is not another way of saying "It's the white folks' fault." Black men must reach beyond our mistrust of the medical system; we must overcome our inclination to refuse help. Our society as a whole must set aside the stigma attached to depression and other mental disorders. None of these things are easily done. Perhaps they won't get done until we open our eyes enough to see the unnecessary and terrible toll depression exacts on African American men and the world around them.

■ ■ ■

It's always strange and sometimes startling to have moments of realization of the damage depression does to me. I see myself diminished, and feel powerless to stop it. I do something or think something, and, having done it or thought it, I say, "That's not me. That's not who I want to be." But it is what I can become.

One such moment of realization was truly frightening. I was out running errands and found a parking space right in front of a store I needed to go into. I drove a car length past it and was about to back in when another car zipped directly into the space. A young white guy got out of the car and hurried into the store. I drove around the corner and immediately found another parking space. I walked to the young man's car and waited.

I confronted him when he came out of the store. "I was backing into this space," I said.

"That's tough," he said as he walked around to the driver's side of his car.

"How did you get to be such an asshole?" I said.

"Yeah, I'm an asshole," he said. "What are you going to do about it?"

Before I knew it I was screaming at the top of my lungs, yelling a stream of obscenities that I had never even whispered in public before.

"Come on around here if you want to get it on," the young man said. "I'm always ready for a fight. I love it."

I've never considered myself a violent person. I'm slow to anger and sparing in shows of emotion of any kind. But at that moment, standing there on the sidewalk, I felt a white-hot rage. I saw the world bathed in that arc-light intensity. I wanted to kill the guy. He smirked, got into his car, and drove away. I stood there still thinking that I wanted to kill him, and fearing that if I had had a gun or some other means of doing it, I would have. This wasn't me.

But what if I were not so far removed from being that kind of person? What if I wasn't a violent person from the outset, but had grown up in an environment where violence was expected? What if I routinely carried a weapon because so many people around me did? If those things were true, and if they were compounded by the impulsiveness, the diminished emotional control, and the failure to reflect on the consequences of an action that can be symptomatic of clinical depression, I could have done something horrible and irrevocable over a parking space. I would have been fully responsible for what I did, but that wouldn't change the fact that it could have been prevented.

Don't misinterpret this story. It's not a warning that depression leads to violence. Quite the contrary, the clinically depressed person is more likely to be a danger to himself than to others. It's true that irritability, clouded thinking, loss of emotional control, and other symptoms of depression can make the sufferer more volatile and vulnerable to being provoked into confrontation. But, like people with other mental disorders, depressed people who get treatment are no more prone to violence than anyone else.

So the story isn't a cautionary tale about depression and violence. Rather, it's about race and depression, and what may happen when the twain meet.

No doubt, the run-in over the parking space was fueled by a surplus of testosterone. But there also was a racial subtext to my confrontation with the rude young man. I can only speculate about how race influenced his behavior. He was too young to remember the era when his white skin would have been enough to earn deference from any black person. I doubt that he was set off because a black person failed to act in a subservient manner toward him. He probably considered himself an equal opportunity jerk, someone who mistreats people without regard to race or national origin. Perhaps subconsciously, however, he viewed black men as inherently threatening, so he went out of his way to make it clear that he wasn't going to let a black man push him around.

For my part, I do remember a time when it would have been inconceivable for me to clash with a white person the way I did that day. I'm ever conscious that those days have passed into history—but did my memories of the era of white supremacy transform this little set-to over a parking space into a very painful and infuriating reopening of old wounds? Did the fact that a white person felt he could figuratively and literally run over my rights with impunity stir in me deep-down doubts about our progress toward racial equality and harmony over the last four decades? And did my depression have anything to do with the existence of those doubts, if those doubts existed at all?

I would answer yes to all those questions.

In physics there is the concept of the "multiplier," a device that intensifies the effect of a force or phenomenon. Similarly, in medicine, there is synergism, when the combined effect of two substances is greater than either substance alone could produce, and also greater than their effects would be when *added* together. The textbook *Maxcy-Rosenan-Last Public Health and Preventive Medicine* explains this "multiplicative" effect with the example of asbestos and smoking: "Asbestos exposure increases the risk of lung cancer 5-fold over the risk of the unexposed person, while smoking increases the risk of lung cancer about 10-fold over the nonsmoker's risk. The asbestos worker who smokes has a risk of about 50 times greater than the person with neither exposure."*

Even though depression falls within the realm of medicine rather than physics, I'll take the liberty of coopting the concept of the multiplier for this discussion; the term is easy to understand and clearly evokes what a black man with depression goes through. I maintain that racism is a multiplier for clinical depression. I believe that the

---

*14th ed.; Robert B. Wallace, and B. N. Doebbeling, eds.

person who is a victim of racism is more susceptible than others are to depression and is in greater danger of suffering a more severe form of the illness.

This is very different from arguing that race alone determines whether a person will suffer from depression and how severe the depression will be. The Surgeon General's Report on Mental Health says studies show no evidence that African Americans as a racial group are more prone to depression than other racial groups. I don't argue with that conclusion. I do indeed argue with the failure to take the next step, which is to determine whether the rate of depression in African Americans is higher in spite of the absence of a genetic predisposition toward depression. Are factors other than genetics at play? I believe they are, and I also believe that racism—because of the double whammy I discussed earlier—is the biggest of the X-factors contributing to depression in black men.

Whatever the cause of clinical depression, the course of the disease is influenced by how we see ourselves and how we believe others see us. The ultimate goal of any treatment is to counter the negativity the depressed person sees in those two images. Racism is about reinforcing our negative self-image and the negative light in which we believe others see us. The presence of racism in our culture and our social atmosphere increases the effect of depression on black men exponentially.

In truth, this is one of those areas in which those who anoint themselves the only ones willing to speak about race forthrightly, without being cowed by political correctness, are getting it wrong. Take, for example, the case of the former *New York Times* reporter Jayson Blair.

A lot was said about race in the aftermath of revelations that Blair fabricated and plagiarized many of his articles, some of which were front-page scoops. Many of those talking were opposed to affirmative action or, at best, were dubious about the value of diversity in the workplace. They charged that top editors at the *Times* overlooked a high rate of reporting errors and other early signs that Blair was not capable of meeting the newspaper's journalistic standards.

The reason this happened, the argument goes, is that Blair is black and the editors were willing to sacrifice all else just to have another black face in the newsroom. In other words, Jayson Blair's race enabled him to do what he did.

What wasn't talked about much was the role racism played in causing Blair to do what he did. I believe racism was a factor. Here's why.

I'm not a psychotherapist, of course—if I were, I would know better than to try to diagnosis a disorder in a person I've never so much as met. But I will take Jayson Blair at his word when he told the New York television station WCBS that what happened at the *Times* "has to do with my own human demons, my own weaknesses, and it ranges from . . . my struggles with substance abuse to my own struggles with mental illness." I take that statement to mean that Blair has been diagnosed, by a professional or by himself, as suffering from a mental disorder.

Add racism, as a multiplier of the mix of mania and depression Blair appears to have been experiencing. A better understanding of the extremes of his professional failings emerges. As a young black man given the opportunity to breathe the rarified air of *The New York Times* he must have felt pressure that would have pushed him hard, even if he were not contending with mental problems. He must have felt he lived in a society that didn't believe he, as an African American man, could succeed. Even as he achieved successes, he probably expected that there were people around him who felt a black man didn't deserve such successes. Going to places where he believed his race made him unwanted, even as an emissary of *The New York Times*, must have been daunting. Blair would have felt the symbiotic dynamic between racism and depression. If racism had instilled in him any doubts of his abilities and his worth, depression would have increased those doubts. If somewhere deep in his subconscious every encounter with a white person seemed to risk racial rejection, depression would have brought it to the surface.

The depression-racism connection doesn't excuse what Jayson Blair did; it only offers part of an explanation of what Blair called "a complicated human tragedy." An estimated 20 million Americans suffer from depression. Whether they are black or white, they find the disease makes life a struggle. It can make going to work difficult, but most manage to do their jobs. No matter what his diagnosis, Jayson Blair is not the poster child for depression in black men. But even if his case is an aberration, it is an extreme example of what can result from the nexus of racism and depression.

Well, doubters might say, if you make so much of racism's effect on depression in black men, doesn't that means as we progress toward a nonracist society, this will become less of a problem, and eventually no problem at all?

Well, yes—as long as one understands that our route to the end of racism and its lingering effects looks more like the up-and-down graph line for the stock market than an arrow-straight path. We take one huge step forward, followed by a series of little steps back. And where we are is much more a matter of individual perception than what's written in the law books. There are moments when Dr. King's Promised Land seems close at hand; there are eternities when it can't be seen from even the highest mountaintop.

I remember something that happened to me in 1970 while I was near the end of my freshman year at Georgia Tech. I had somehow missed out on getting into an on-campus dorm room for the next quarter. The housing office tried to help by giving me a list of nearby apartments that catered to Tech students. One of the places was in a great location, just off campus. A woman answered when I called. She said the building was dormitory-style housing. The rent she quoted was reasonable. There were two rooms available, she said, and I could come look them over and see if one of them was what I had in mind. Perfect, I thought, as I rushed out the door.

A white woman, gray-haired and well on her way from matronly to elderly, answered my knock at the resident manager's door. "Yes?" she said, eyeing me suspiciously through the partially opened door.

"I spoke to you on the phone a few minutes ago about the rooms," I said.

"What?" she said, followed by "What? What?" Each "What?" was uttered with increasing incredulity.

Maybe she was hard of hearing. I repeated myself.

"You're a student at Tech?" she asked. Her question was delivered with the tone of a person who already knows what the answer is going to be and has decided in advance not to believe it.

"Yes," I said. "I got your number from the student housing office."

"Well, somebody made a mistake," she said, her voice taking on a high, strained quality. "We don't have any rooms left. They're all taken."

"I believe I spoke to you," I said, thinking, "Unless it was a member of the huge office staff you've got living with you in this tiny apartment."

"No," she said, her voice rising near the register that only dogs can hear. "There's been a mistake. We don't have any rooms available." Then she closed the door.

I left there seething. What had happened was so transparent. She gets a call from a Tech student who was referred to her by the housing office. Sure, she says. We've got rooms. Come on over. But, wouldn't you know, it was her bad luck that one of the dozen or so African American students at Tech (she probably had no idea there were any) showed up at her door.

Discouraged and angry—the anger was definitely dominating—I decided not to let this pass. I went to a white student with whom I had struck up a friendship. "I need to borrow your skin," I said.

"What?" he said.

I explained what had happened. "I need somebody white to go over there and see if she shows the rooms," I said.

"Maybe she really made a mistake and there aren't any rooms," he said.

I didn't know if he was really that incredibly naïve, just reluctant to get involved in this mess, or both. "This is one way to find out," I said.

"Okay," he said. "I'll do it."

Later in the day, he called and asked about renting a room. "What did she say?" I asked when he hung up the phone.

"She said come over and she would see if she could help me," he said.

"Nothing about two rooms?"

"Nope."

Was she gun-shy after the shock of this morning? I wondered. Or did she really not have the rooms available? No way, I thought. She wouldn't waste someone's time, or her own time, meeting to discuss a nonexistent room. "Okay," I said. "You better get over there."

While my friend was on his errand, I waited with a sense of excitement. I wasn't just taking a racist rebuff. I was doing something about it, and I was doing it in what I thought was a clever way. My coconspirator finally returned. His face was blank. "Well?" I said.

He shook his head. "Man, she greased you. When I got there she said she had two rooms. She showed them to me. When I told her I had to think about it, she asked for my phone number so she could call me in case someone else rented a room and there was only one left. She's really messing with you."

I immediately went back and knocked on her door. She opened it a crack. "Yes?" she said.

"I was here this morning," I said. "You told me you didn't have any rooms."

She opened the door wider. "That's right," she said, sounding more confident than ever.

"Then why did you tell a white friend of mine who was over here a few minutes ago that you have two rooms?" I said. My voice was under control but edged with anger. "Why did you show him two empty rooms?"

"What? What? What?" Again with the escalating "What"s.

"Don't you know it's against the law to discriminate in housing?" I said. "Don't you know I can sue you for this?"

"I don't discriminate against nobody!" she screeched. "I got students from all over the world staying here. I treat everybody the same!"

"Then why did you lie to me?"

"I made a mistake," she said. "I misunderstood. You can look at the rooms. You can come in and pick the one you want. Come on and I'll show you." Her voice was pleading now, frightened.

She couldn't get my name on the lease fast enough. She fawned over me as if I were the Prodigal Son returned. In the early moments of victory over racism, I was exultant. She was an old woman; I was a young man. Her ways were the ways of the past; mine were the path to the future. Time and the law were on my side.

But not too long after those heady moments, I came back down to reality. The veil of bigotry that she had dropped between us in that first encounter had not been discarded; it had only been parted slightly. Yes, she soon would be gone, but the things that made her fear and hate me would survive her. I was certain even then that they would survive me. I went from the jubilation of the general who has won the war to the weariness of the infantryman who survives one battle only to trudge on to the next. Some might argue that mine was a pessimistic view, but history has proven me right. There are fair-housing agencies today that send "testers" out to see whether racial discrimination still limits where black Americans can rent apartments or buy houses. Invariably, they report that the problem persists. What can I say about this state of affairs these thirty years after my run-in with a racist landlord whose time even back then was supposed to be long past?

It's depressing.

■ ■ ■

I consider how depression has affected me and then try to extrapolate to the effects on black men who share my adversities and enjoy none of my advantages. Advocates for people with mental illness have to fight every day against the stigmatizing idea that people who suffer from mental illness are prone to violence and criminal behavior. They rightly argue that violence and criminality are not the natural consequences of mental illness, but can result when mental illness remains untreated and those with mental illness live in an environment that spawns antisocial behavior. This is what happens to too many black men who suffer from depression. There is a failure to treat the illness, and there is an environment that can make the consequences of that failure catastrophic.

There are many ways to measure the impact of depression. By one estimate, between $35 billion and $44 billion is spent on the treatment of depression in the United States each year. Depression is blamed for 200 million lost workdays each year, making it the leading cause of workplace absenteeism in this country, according to the Surgeon General's Report. A study published in the *Journal of the American Medical Association* in June 2003 placed a $31 billion price tag on workplace productivity lost to depression. Depression is second only to heart disease in disabling American workers. The illness also is the leading cause of disability in the world, according to the World Health Organization.

Such statistics show the impact of depression on general populations. Now think what it would be like to face adverse effects many times worse: that's what it's like for black men if racism has the multiplier effect on depression that I believe it does.

The Surgeon General's report adds,

Although only a minority seek professional help to relieve a mood disorder, depressed people are significantly more likely than others to visit a physician for some other reason. Depression-related visits to physicians thus account for a large portion of health care expenditures. Seeking another or less stigmatized explanation for their difficulties, some depressed patients undergo extensive and expensive diagnostic procedures and then get treated for various other complaints while the mood disorder goes undiagnosed and untreated.

Measuring the impact of depression is meaningless to those who suffer depression in self-imposed isolation, as African American men are apt to do. We refuse to acknowledge membership in such statistical cohorts. Our pain is intensely personal. But even that pain, and the hurt we inflict on others in our anguish, are not the measure of the ultimate price we pay for depression. They are preludes. All too often, we ultimately pay with our lives.

⬛ FOUR ⬛

Moving Black Suicide Out of the Shadows

Blues, blues, blues, why did you bring trouble to me?
Oh, Death, please sting me and take me out of my misery.
——Clarence Williams and Sara Martin,
"Death Sting Me Blues"

Among African American men—and in the black community in general—the response to suicide is something beyond benign silence. Suicide is treated with outright hostility and denial. The strong religious taboo against the act is one of the reasons. To acknowledge that someone has killed himself is to adjudge him hell-bound. But more than spiritual considerations lead black men to rationalize suicide as a "white thing." The very idea that African American men would take their own lives is an affront to our people's history and experiences in this country. How could we have in our blood the collective strengths that allowed blacks to survive three centuries of oppression, only to wind up killing ourselves? (Of course, this idea overlooks the role of suicide in the earliest stage of the slave experience, when Africans jumped to their deaths from the slave ships.)

The civil rights leader who told me he believed African Americans didn't start suffering from depression until segregation ended had similar feelings about suicide: "Black folks didn't kill themselves before integration," he said. "There was only one black man in Atlanta who committed suicide before the late 1960s."

He didn't qualify the statement in any way. He was saying that there was only one suicide by a black man in the entire history of Atlanta. And he was saying it with certainty. He even knew the man's name and the circumstances of this death. "He had lots of businesses but he lived beyond his means," he said. "Money troubles finally got to be too much." I didn't say anything.

Then he leaned back from the table a bit, obviously in thought. After a moment, he said, "There was one other black man in Atlanta that I know of who killed himself. This man was a doctor. He was mixed up about his sexuality." (It used to be that many African Americans thought homosexuality was the only "reasonable" reason for a black man to take his own life. I remember that when a successful black entertainer killed himself in the 1970s, the friend who gave me the news said, "You know he did it because he was funny." Indeed, there had been a rumor that the entertainer was gay. This attitude about gay black men and suicide wasn't rooted in homophobia alone. It was based more on the idea that homosexuals were weak and not real men, and real black men didn't kill themselves.)

My tablemate came up with one more name, that of a Miami man whom he had known personally. "That's very few," he said. "Black men don't usually do that stuff."

Black men do die from suicide, of course, and we are doing so at an increasing rate, even if you ignore the likely undercounting of black suicides. The suicide rate among black men has increased by nearly 50 percent since 1980. And, according to the Centers for Disease Control and Prevention, the rate at which black men aged fifteen to nineteen killed themselves increased by 146 percent between 1980 and 1995, while the increase for white males the same age was 22 percent. (Meanwhile, statistics consistently show that young black women have a suicide rate among the lowest of any American demographic group studied. Why do young African American men and women who come out of the same cultures and share the same life experiences differ so much in the rates at which they take their own lives? This is worth serious investigation.)

While widely accepted statistics show that white men still commit suicide more frequently than black men, the gap is closing. There are theories about why—such as that black men are devastated when we learn that affluence and equal opportunity are not all they were cracked up to be—but, again, as Alvin Poussaint points out, there are precious few data to support any theory.

In fact, Dr. Poussaint argues, suicides among African American men are not scrutinized closely enough to say with confidence what the suicide rate actually is. The unreliability of those statistics is the result of factors beyond those that make official counts of suicides in general questionable, Dr. Poussaint says. Just as whites do, African Americans who lose relatives or loved ones to possible suicide provide information to authorities to support any conclusion other than suicide. And, just as whites do, blacks sometimes complete suicide in ways intended to look like accidents. It's easy to believe the person who died after a fall from a high place didn't jump; he just lost his footing while fooling around up there. Even death from a self-inflicted gunshot wound can be rationalized as a reckless game of Russian roulette. The more unacceptable suicide is to the survivors, the more they accept alternative explanations for a suspicious death. Because of the increased stigma attached to suicide in black communities, such efforts to deny or hide self-killing are probably more common than among whites.

In *Lay My Burden Down*, his book about black suicide, Dr. Poussaint makes a strong case for counting as suicides some deaths that are never considered suicide. He isn't talking only about the "suicide by cop" I mentioned earlier. He also would treat high-risk behaviors that can lead to death—such as drug abuse and unsafe sex—as slow suicides. If Dr. Poussaint's methodology were adopted, the official suicide rate for black men certainly would be dramatically higher. But that's not likely to happen anytime soon. Would someone who is in so much despair that he wants to end his life be willing to endure the misery of a long, drawn-out death from, say, AIDS or drug addiction? I'm sure most people can't conceive of it, but of course, that doesn't mean it doesn't happen. (Andrew Solomon, in his comprehensive book *The Noonday Demon: An Atlas of Depression* recounts his experience of falling so deeply into depression that he attempted to contract AIDS so he would have a socially acceptable reason for suicide. Had he succeeded—he didn't—contracting AIDS through unsafe sex would have been considered the reason for his suicide instead of what it was: the first step in the act of suicide itself.)

While there may be gaps in the information gathering, there are more than enough data to debunk the African American community's collective denial of suicide among black men. Our people's history has not inoculated us against self-killing, or made us immune to it. I know from personal experience.

■ ■ ■

I remember when I came close to killing myself. My momentum toward that moment began early in 1995, in the midst of what I recall as a winter of rain. I was forty-four years old and adrift. My wife, Claire, and I were separated. I saw my sons only on the weekends. Fleeing from my family was my way of dealing with unrelenting unhappiness. They were not the source of my unhappiness: They were victims of it. I knew that in my heart. I also knew the unhappiness came from something deep inside me, something I couldn't leave behind no matter where I went. The depression had been there through more than twenty tortured years. But I still didn't have a name for it. "Clinical depression" was not yet a part of my vocabulary.

Every day was gloomy, the air filled with a chilling wetness. The sky was constantly an opaque gray, denying me light and its life-giving energy.

But this weather report may not be accurate. It likely is a reflection of the meteorology of my mind. The gloominess, the chill, the energy-robbing grayness were not the weather I encountered outside. They were what I carried around inside me.

Atlanta is a city that doesn't allow winter to overstay its welcome, and winter isn't much welcomed in the first place. Spring is invited in as early as possible. It makes the world green and bright. In spite of its mania for development, Atlanta bills itself as "the City of Trees." When spring comes, those trees sprout buds and the beginning of the leaves that will cool and soothe us in the summer. Atlanta doesn't go too far into spring before everything begins to flower, from daffodils to dogwoods. The area is treated to a riot of blossoms. Spring was always a tonic for me, a time of beauty and joy and hope.

I know the time when I contemplated suicide lapped over into spring, but I recall none of the wonders of the season. For me, it was just the opposite: no beauty, no joy, no hope. While those around me luxuriated in the fledgling rays of early spring sunshine, I dwelled in a deep and bleak pit. The pit had walls as smooth as glass. Every day started with the seemingly impossible task of climbing out of that hole. From the moment I tried to get out of bed in the morning, I had the sensation of beginning to rise out of the darkness, only to fall back in. This debilitating, draining mood made even the simplest undertaking a struggle. As soon as I got home from work, I fell back into the pit of my own accord, willingly sliding back into the deep darkness, the oblivion, the nothingness, because "nothing" was about as much as I could handle. Sometimes I was unable to sleep, thinking of the many things that were out of joint in my life. At other times sleep was inevitable and immediate; I sank into it as surely as a heavy stone drops into the ocean. I invariably awakened in the wee hours. By the time I finally began drifting back toward sleep, the alarm had sounded with a bullying insistence, the final interruption of a night of fitful slumber. I was back in the pit, only it was deeper than the day before.

Suicidal thoughts are not uncommon among people who suffer depression. Studies show that about 15 percent of Americans think seriously of killing themselves at some point in their lives. During some of my previous lows, the idea of ending it all had come into my mind. My favored fantasy was death by automobile. There I would be, driving down the expressway, doing my customary ten miles per hour above the speed limit, and I would think, "What if I just swerved off the road and slammed full-speed into that overpass support column? It would look as if I fell asleep and lost control of the car. And nobody would ever know what really happened." That was important to me. I didn't want anyone to know I had taken my own life.

But back then suicide had been just one on the list of options for dealing with what I was going through. It was at the bottom of the list by a long way; on reflection, I could easily see that it was the most ridiculous option, and the only one that was irrevocable. I really didn't want that finality. I had a strong survival instinct. No matter how bad things had gotten, I had hope that they would get better, as they always had. I wanted to live to see the better times ahead.

Self-preservation can yield to a certain amount of psychic pain, however. I was reaching that level of mental suffering as I retreated into my apartment/cave. I had always had a well-deserved reputation as a loner. One of my fondest childhood memories is of getting out of bed at daybreak on summer mornings, well before anyone else in the house awakened. I would tiptoe out and run to some woods nearby. I had found a clearing where I would sit, surrounded by trees that rose up like the walls of a cathedral. There, in the quiet and the glow of first light, I exulted in my solitude.

Yet solitude had become a form of torture for me by the time of that gray Atlanta spring. I wanted more than anything to be left alone, but I felt desperately lonely. The silence of the apartment was a constant echo in my head. I was probing the depths of that pit as never before, and this time I had no hope of pulling myself out. I thought about suicide more often than ever. The fantasy of a staged car accident was gone. If I did it, I wanted people to know I had done it.

George Orwell's novel *Nineteen Eighty-four* defines "doublethink" as "the power of holding two contradictory beliefs in one's mind simultaneously, and accepting both of them." Some of us know you don't need Big Brother's methods to produce doublethink. The troubled mind is apt to hold contradictory thoughts at the same instant. I was double-thinking about suicide: If I kill myself, I thought, everyone will be better off without me. Running on a parallel track in my mind was this train of thought: They'll miss me, and they'll be sorry. So, on the one hand, by killing myself I would commit an act of selfless sacrifice; on the other hand, I would mete out suffering, taking a vindictive revenge. Both ideas couldn't be true.

But my wounded mind had no interest in puzzling through what could and couldn't be true. I was doing a lot of things as if on automatic pilot, barely remembering what I had done afterward. That's the way I recall that dreary Saturday. I wandered aimlessly around the apartment, if moving about such a small place can be called wandering. Then, for some reason, I climbed the stairs and went to the bedroom closet. There was a length of rope there. I had bought it to tie down furniture during the move to the apartment. I uncoiled it and draped it over the balcony. I looked down and saw that part of the rope lay on the floor. Too long, I thought. I slowly pulled the rope up, hand over hand, until the other end was about where I wanted it. I securely tied my end to the balcony railing.

I went downstairs and walked under the rope, whose end dangled just above my head. The kitchen table was a few steps away. I pulled out one of the chairs and placed it beneath the rope. I stood up on the chair. I held the end of the rope with my hands apart, measuring out a length of it. Yes, there was enough to make a loop. This would do it.

I don't remember exactly what I was thinking at that crucial moment. Not much of anything, I believe. I didn't have a rush of thoughts. My mind was almost empty. My life wasn't flashing before my eyes. I didn't look back and call up memories of good times. Neither was I thinking about my miseries. I wasn't weighing the good against the bad, with my life in the balance. If the scale tips toward the good, do I live? If it tips toward the bad, do I die? No, I wasn't thinking like that. I wasn't even trying to make a decision.

No decision was necessary. What I was doing had an inevitability that I could not overcome. What would happen would happen. It was as if I were making a journey that required me to walk along a high mountain ledge. Sometimes the ledge would be comfortably wide; sometimes it would be dangerously narrow. Somehow I had gotten so intent on the trip that I didn't even look down at the path. I knew when it got very narrow because I would teeter and almost fall. But I didn't control the ledge that held me up. I just walked, and when the ledge got too narrow to walk on, I would fall. That would be that.

Around the world each day, untold millions of people reach this point. They hold in their hands a length of rope or a loaded gun or something else that, in their despair, they believe to be the lethal cure for their suffering. The civilized world looks aghast at America's homicide rate, but our suicide rate is almost 50 percent higher. The Surgeon General's 1999 "Call to Action to Prevent Suicide" reported that 31,000 Americans killed themselves in 1996. About 500,000 more were treated in emergency rooms as a result of suicide attempts. Not all depressed people complete the act of suicide. Not all suicides are depressed. But untreated depression is the greatest predictor of suicide. Between 10 and 15 percent of patients hospitalized for severe depression end their lives in suicide. An estimated 20 to 35 percent of the people who kill themselves have major depressive disorder. Depression twists the mind until suicide seems to make sense. For many who reach this point, it is the final step. It is the irrational end of a tortured journey.

For some reason, that day I stepped away. I stepped down from the chair and looked at the rope. I hadn't made a noose. I wondered why I had done what I did. I rationalized that it was nothing more than the old suicide fantasy, taken to a different level. Instead of imagining suicide, I was acting it out, going through the motions to see what it took to do it, but with no intention of actually doing it. But I knew in my heart that that wasn't true, that my rationalization made no sense. And even if it were true, my behavior still frightened me. I couldn't comprehend why I had done it, but I wanted to grasp it. For the first time in a long time, instead of thinking only about how miserable I was, I started to try to think about how I had gotten that way. My first visit to Dr. Serravezza was still a couple of months away, but my brush with suicide pointed me toward treatment.

Unlike what happens for too many others, that day wasn't the end of a journey for me; it was the beginning of one. I didn't know where that journey would take me. Perhaps I was on the road to more days like this one, when I would stare over into the abyss until, finally, there was nothing left in me to stop me from taking the plunge. Or perhaps I was on a path toward understanding what I had been and what I was becoming. I told myself that I should hope for the latter.

But first, of course, I had to find a reason for hope.

◼ ◼ ◼

African Americans tend to believe that we have that reason for hope embedded in our souls, and that mining enough of it to ward off the impulse toward suicide involves a little digging within ourselves. There's reason to believe this. Through slavery, through the virtual serfdom of sharecropping, through the rule of Jim Crow, through the use of unjust laws and vigilante violence in attempts to deny us the most basic rights of citizenship, through racism in all its evil manifestations, most black Americans have never given up on themselves or this country. We have believed that we will reach the Promised Land that Dr. Martin Luther King, Jr., spoke of into the last days of his life, and we have held on to the hope that America will one day be the land of freedom and equality it promises to be.

Even so, we're fooling ourselves if we believe that being a people with a history of hope makes us immune to suicide. We're fooling ourselves, because we are not immune to depression, which is the clearest indicator of the possibility of suicide. There is no doubt that hopefulness is one of health's helpmates. Studies have shown that an optimistic outlook promotes good physical health, while pessimism is detrimental to good health. Positive thinking doesn't protect us from all ills and injuries, however. Happy people can come down with cancer, develop ailments that are handed down genetically, break their arms, or suffer any other of the many afflictions of the flesh. The same is true of any mental illness. In the case of depression, the brain may be affected by a chemical imbalance, a genetic defect, an injury, or other possible causes. As with any other disease, we are not inoculated from depression even if a wellspring of hope handed down from generation to generation flows in our blood.

Understanding this truth about depression is key to understanding the crisis in suicide among African American men. I use the word "crisis" because black men are dying unnecessarily, dying because of ignorance and shame. The problem is critical among the young black men who have experienced the previously noted explosion in their suicide rate in recent years. A theory to explain that increase has been bandied about in the media: African American men, it's suggested, have found that the gains made as a result of the civil rights movement aren't what they were cracked up to be. There are added responsibilities and there is the realization that we can fail even if we're given equal opportunities. The theory says, in effect, that we're unable to cope with success. This may be a well-intentioned attempt to explain a problem, but it winds up being one of the micro insults Carl Bell talks about. With no evidence to support it, the theory is tantamount to telling blacks that we were better off when racism kept us in our place.

I don't buy it.

A more likely and reasonable explanation for the problem requires a realization of why the risk of suicide rises for anyone suffering from depression. Finding a reason for hope is difficult for anyone with clinical depression. If the depressed person's wait for the end of hopelessness goes on too long, if the attendant pain becomes too much to bear, the slide toward suicide takes on a logic of inevitability that it really should not have. The depressed person reasons that we all die eventually. If every moment of putting off the inevitable only leads to another moment of misery, well, then, why continue to put it off?

If depression fosters this kind of thinking about death, consider what it would do to the thinking of black men. We are bombarded with statistics and stereotypes telling us that of all the inevitable deaths, ours may be the most inevitable. We have a greater risk of premature death. We're more likely to die as a result of violence, particularly gun violence. For too many young black men, the real and perceived vulnerability to violence is an invitation to take advantage of the easy access to guns as an means of self-protection. Possession of a gun, of course, is a major step up the ladder of risk factors for completed suicide.

For young men who accept the message that they are doomed to die early and who believe society values their lives less than those of others, it becomes even more likely that a descent into depression will allow the illogic of the inevitability of suicide to take hold. When these young men live in an environment in which guns—the most effective means of suicide—are readily available, it should be no surprise that a suicide crisis develops.

Attention has focused recently on the problem of suicide among young black men. This is a good thing, a necessary step toward breaking the silence about suicide in African American communities. However, it would be a mistake if this media focus created the perception that the problem of suicide among black men is limited to the young, especially those who live in poverty and in environments of violence. The truth is that economic status for black men is not an impenetrable shield against depression and suicide. The most successful among us can be at risk. Consider Razak Bello's story.

On a November morning in 1994, Bello dropped his wife, Kenya, off at her job. It was a big day for the couple, who had been married for just short of six months. Razak was on his way to a job interview arranged by Andrew Young, who had served as a top aide to Dr. Martin Luther King, Jr., as a congressman, as the U.S. ambassador to the United Nations, and as mayor of Atlanta. Young, who is also a minister, had performed the Bellos' wedding. This was the kind of connection the twentysomething couple had. Kenya is the daughter of George Napper, who was Atlanta's first black police chief and later the city's public safety commissioner. Razak graduated from Morehouse College, one of the nation's most prestigious historically black colleges. Among the school's alumni are Dr. King and Maynard

Jackson, Atlanta's first African American mayor. Being a "Morehouse man" carries a certain cachet. For generations, the students at the all-male school have had drilled into them the idea that they always must carry themselves with a mixture of self-assurance and dignity. They have been taught that while on campus and once out in the community, a Morehouse man acts on an ethos of fulfilling duties and living up to responsibilities. Former classmates considered Razak Bello the quintessential Morehouse man. When he graduated he landed a job with Coca-Cola that positioned him to begin climbing the corporate ladder.

That November morning should have been one of excited expectation for Razak and Kenya Bello, but it wasn't. When Razak told her "I love you" and drove away, Kenya could only look after him and hope for the best. She had had to talk him into going to the interview. He didn't believe he could get through it. The twenty-seven-year-old man who once seemed capable of accomplishing anything he set his mind to was fighting an illness of the mind that convinced him that he could accomplish absolutely nothing.

For years, Razak Bello had suffered from bipolar disorder, also known as manic depression; he had been diagnosed and began treatment only a year earlier. Kenya had learned that he was sick about a year before they were married. It didn't change the fact that she loved him and believed he was the man with whom she would spend the rest of her life. She thought that, as his wife, she would be at the center of a support system that would help Razak recover and become the man of achievement he was destined to be. But no one—not Razak Bello, and not the people who loved him—realized what a devious enemy he was up against.

As his illness progressed, Razak's swings between the manic phases of energetic excitement and the depressed phases of listless despair became more extreme. Kenya remembers that while they were driving to the airport one day, Razak began looking about excitedly and warning her that she shouldn't let the people in the airplanes flying high above see them. Eventually, he had to be hospitalized and put on medication. He didn't want anyone at Coke to know about these problems: He feared it would cost him his job. But the illness that sapped his energy and confused his thinking left him incapable of doing his work in international distribution. Kenya learned her husband's job was in jeopardy when she heard through the grapevine that a meeting to decide Razak's fate was scheduled at Coke's corporate headquarters. She went to the meeting uninvited to defend her "Zak."

"There I was," she says, "walking into this meeting of top-level Coke managers who were talking about what to do with Zak. I went in there pleading with them that Zak was not on [illegal] drugs. I said he was a person with a condition that he was dealing with. I told them he was a person of good character and that they knew he was a person of good character. They knew that Zak had stellar job performance evaluations up until that point. They knew all of that."

It didn't do any good. After a two-week hospitalization for his illness, Razak returned home to find a letter from Coke. "They fired him anyway," Kenya Bello says.

Kenya remembers this as the point at which her husband's downward spiral appeared to become irreversible. He refused to take his medication. This happens with many people who suffer from depression or manic depression. They are frustrated by the side effects of the medicine, while not seeing a quick improvement in their condition. Some "feel better" (either because the medication is working or because they are beginning a manic phase) and decide they don't need the medicine at all. Kenya knew it was essential that Razak continue to take his medication, but nothing she said would convince him to do so.

The night before her husband was scheduled to go to the job interview set up by Andy Young, Kenya Bello prayed. Prayer was not unusual for her, but it was different this time. "I didn't ask God to give Zak the job or to make everything turn out the way we wanted," Kenya told me almost nine years later. "I just asked Him to help me accept whatever happened, to give me the strength to bear what might come. That was the first time I prayed about things in that way."

The next morning, when her husband dropped her off and headed for his big job interview, Kenya hoped that when he returned to pick her up after work he would greet her with his old smile of confidence and excitement. She imagined that he would tell her the interview had gone great and he had gotten the job on the spot. He would be energized and excited about life again, ready to do whatever it took to capitalize on this new momentum and keep moving forward.

But that didn't happen. Razak wasn't there to pick her up at the end of the workday. She waited three hours before leaving for her parents' house, where the Bellos lived. There was a knock on the door that night: the police, with the worst possible news.

Razak had gone to the Atlanta Marriott Marquis, one of the city's tonier hotels. The Marquis has a huge atrium rising floor after floor above the lobby. At about three P.M., Razak got off an elevator on the thirty-second floor. He mounted the safety railing and dived off, screaming all the way down. He hit one of the hotel's clear bubble elevators before landing in the lobby fountain. He was dead when paramedics reached him a few minutes later.

Kenya Bello was devastated, but thankfully she did not feel the anger and shame common among people left behind by the suicide of someone they love. These feelings are especially frequent in a culture like African Americans', where we are taught that depression and other mental illnesses are character flaws and suicide is the ultimate sign of weakness. Kenya knew that her husband's character wasn't flawed and that he wasn't weak. He suffered from a disease, a mental illness. She also knew that he loved her up until his dying moment. He'd put a note on her computer the day he died: "I deceived you and everyone else. I can't live with myself any longer. All I know is that I love you."

Yet in spite of everything Kenya knew about his illness, she had never even considered that he might take his own life. She knew her husband had an inner core of strength that was reinforced by his family and friends. "He was the last person I would have thought would kill himself," she told me. "It just never crossed my mind."

Despite that, Kenya believes that her prayer the night before Razak's death was God's way of preparing her for the grief that would come.

Kenya Napper Bello is an amazing young woman. Intelligent, energetic, and determined, she has transformed her personal tragedy into a public calling. She has not gone quietly into widowhood. Instead, she has become a crusader. She speaks out about her experience to break the silence surrounding suicide, especially in the black community. She freely admits that she and others around Razak didn't recognize the depth and danger of his illness. But ultimately, she says, she is convinced that when her husband sought medical treatment, he didn't get the kind of treatment that would have saved his life. He should have been diagnosed earlier, she believes. And she wonders if things would have been different if she and Razak had known then what she knows now, if they had known what they were up against. Perhaps they could have found a more effective medication that her husband would have stayed on.

"Razak died of a poorly treated, deteriorating medical condition," Kenya wrote in an article for *Essence* magazine. "That it was a mental illness makes his death no different from death from cancer or diabetes. As his widow, I have no anger or shame. His essence was golden—I am honored to have been his wife. Yet I am deeply anguished to have discovered, far too late, that his beautiful life might have been saved."

It can take a lot to prevent someone with severe depression from resorting to suicide. For numerous reasons, the difficulty is even greater when the person suffering is a black man. There are hints of that in what happened to Razak Bello. But John Wilson's tragic story makes it crystal clear.

Wilson, the chairman of the Washington, D.C., city council, had everything in place that should have enabled him to survive his depression. He was seeing a psychiatrist and taking medication. Four recent suicide attempts had warned his doctor, his wife, and a close circle of friends that Wilson was at a crisis point and that drastic action was needed. They wanted him hospitalized until he was stable and taking effective medication that would prevent him from harming himself.

Wilson refused to be treated, for the same reason that most people in our society would refuse: He didn't want to be stuck with the stigma of depression and suicide attempts. If word got out that he was seriously depressed, that he was taking medication for it, that he had attempted suicide and had had to enter a mental hospital for treatment, Wilson believed he would be finished politically. And all this couldn't have come at a worse time for him. He was preparing to run for mayor in an effort to fulfill his dream of leading the city he loved. To those who urged him to quietly enter a hospital outside Washington so that his stay might be kept secret, Wilson offered assurances that to take that risk was not necessary. He said he had emerged from dangerous periods of depression before and he could do it again. He had the willpower to resist suicide, he said. He wanted his secret kept at all costs.

His depression had been a well-kept secret for many years, in fact. By outward appearances Wilson had little reason to be depressed. He had come to Washington in the 1960s, while he was still in his twenties and already well known within civil rights circles as an activist who had been an effective operative since he joined the movement as a college student. He took up the cause of home rule for the District. When the D.C. council was formed, he was elected one of the original members. At thirty-one, he also was the youngest. He established himself as a brilliant street politician and a master tactician within the halls of power. He became the council's leading expert on the district's budget. He introduced more legislation than any other member, and he had the skill to get most of it passed. He regularly won reelection with 80 percent majorities in one of Washington's most diverse districts. He seemed destined to become mayor.

Yet there were very public signs that all was not well. In spite of his record of one easy victory after another, the approach of election day always brought out in Wilson expressions of self-doubt and anxiety. He often questioned whether he'd ever accomplished anything worthwhile and threatened to quit politics in frustration. Several times he did announce that he was quitting, only to change his mind. He sometimes exploded at colleagues for little or no reason. He made outrageous statements and behaved erratically. These things didn't set off alarm bells for most people. If anything, they added to Wilson's appeal, setting him apart from cautious, cookie-cutter politicians who were careful about every word they said and every move they made. Only those very close to Wilson saw such actions for what they were, symptoms of the depression that was tightening its grip on him as time went by.

One of those closest to Wilson believed that being a black man whose achievements outstripped anything he had ever been told or imagined he could reach played a role in his depression. "John had to struggle with his identity in the sense of 'What in the world am I doing here? What have I done to deserve being where I am?' " Wayne "Red" Miles, Wilson's friend since elementary school, told *The Washington Post*. Accepting that he had earned his success was more difficult for a black man like Wilson, Miles said, because "with most nonblacks, there is a generation or so to fall back upon, like 'Hey, my daddy had some big job,' or maybe 'my granddaddy.' But here was John Wilson, and he was just like a flower that appeared in the desert."

John Wilson only spoke publicly about his depression once, when he addressed a meeting of the Washington, D.C., Mental Health Association. The following description is based on *The Washington Post*'s report of the event.

Wilson described himself as "a person who deals with depression, a very painful, very difficult disease . . . [that] leads to a great feeling of being lost, of a hole in your body." He added that the illness was doing terrible damage among blacks: "I believe that more people are dying from depression than are dying of AIDS, heart trouble, high blood pressure, anything else, simply because I believe depression brings on all those diseases."

To demonstrate the vulnerability of young people in the black community to depression and suicide, Wilson recounted this experience to the audience of mental health professionals: One day he overheard a group of boys in his neighborhood talking about different kinds and colors of metals and crushed velvet. Wilson thought they were talking about cars. He recently had had his car stolen from in front of his house, so he asked them for some advice. "What's the best kind of car to buy that nobody wants to steal?" he said. The answer he got was laughter.

"They said, 'We're not talking about cars,'" Wilson explained, "'We're talking about caskets—what kind of caskets we want to be buried in.'

"Suicide," Wilson added. "It's the number one killer among young black people, but we call it gunfire. . . . Our kids are not crazy. They're not a generation of lost people. They're a generation of people that need mental health treatment to deal with depression because there's so much in this world they can never have, and they know they will never have it, and it's putting them in a grand funk. . . .

"When you find people who are well educated, have everything this world has to offer, and they're suffering from depression, think about the kid who's living in public housing with a lot of other losers. He's supposed to come out and act like a nice middle-class kid? Well, he's not going to do that unless there's a miracle . . . and somebody picks him up and puts him together. . . . We have to begin understanding the people who suffer from this disease. Most of them are harmless to you, but extremely harmful to themselves and very dangerous to the community itself. . . . They are young people that will drive drunk. They are the young people who will drive by and shoot somebody. It's not just meanness. It's 'What is the purpose of existence?' That is the question that they ask themselves. Why am I existing? What is my reason for existing?"

The people Wilson was talking about were young black men, of course. And the question he must have heard from them in his bones was this: What reason do we have to live?

In May of 1993, less than two weeks after he made those remarks, John Wilson succumbed to depression and gave up his many reasons for living. He hanged himself in the basement of his home. He was forty-nine.

Throughout our history in this country, African American men have had reason to fear that death stalks us. When our minds and our resolve are clouded by depression, we can give up resisting it. We can welcome death; we can embrace it. It may happen when we have no prospect of achieving anything. It may happen just as we begin living up to our potential for achievement. And it may happen when we have achieved much, but remain nagged by doubts that we deserve any of it. Whenever suicides happen, they happen in spite of our ability to prevent them. All these lives are worth saving. American society as a whole has a role to play in preventing suicides by black men. But the crucial role belongs to the black community itself. Before we can find solutions, we've got to start talking openly about the problem.

Dr. Donna Barnes, a sociologist whose son was a suicide victim, has dedicated herself to fighting suicide among African Americans. She is a founder and president of the National Organization for People of Color Against Suicide (NOPCAS) in Washington, D.C. Dr. Barnes told me there are special challenges in stemming the rising tide of suicide among young black men: "They need to understand that they don't have to try to be macho in the face of everything that confronts them in their lives. What we need is to have support groups to teach these young men how to become men in ways that say it's okay to talk about your pain. They have to learn how to talk about their depression."

That applies to black men of all ages.

FIVE

If You're Black, Go Around Back

Oh, I'm shipwrecked, shipwrecked and ain't got time to lose.
Lawd, if someone don't save me I'll go down singin' the ship-
wrecked blues.

—Spencer Williams,
"Shipwrecked Blues"

In America, we have two mental health care systems, separate and unequal.
You gain access to one by going in through the front door—the door
for those with wealth or good health insurance. This system emphasizes early intervention in treating mental illnesses such as depression. It provides psychotherapy and medication as long as they are
needed.

You get into the other system through the back door, and you are
treated accordingly. This system is for those who are poor and/or
among the nation's 40 million uninsured. Most often, patients don't
enter this system until their illnesses have reached a serious stage.
The usual points of entry include hospital emergency rooms, homeless shelters, and jails and prisons. If psychotherapy and medication
are made available at all in this system, it is only for a limited time.
The people who use this lower-tier mental health system look like
America—they are men, women, and children from diverse racial,
religious, and ethnic groups. But black men suffering from depres-

sion make up a disproportionate number of those who enter treatment through the back door.

Part of the problem is our own fault. We, as black men, tend to ignore our emotional problems. When we suffer from depression or anger disorders, for example, we tend to act as if inaction is the cure. It's like our refusal to see doctors for physical ailments—remember the study showing African American men are less likely than white men to visit a doctor before they're in poor health—only worse. The vast majority of those who enter the mental health care system's front door do so voluntarily. In contrast, many who get treatment through the back door do so because they have no choice.

However, the back door has been opened wider for black men. The primary reason is that America's jails and prisons are used as repositories for people with mental illness. African American men, who wind up behind bars in disproportionate numbers, have been caught in the nation's tide of incarcerated people with mental disorders.

African American men also are more likely to be treated for acute illness or injury in emergency rooms, where mental illness often is diagnosed as a coincident condition. Shelters are struggling to help the high percentage of the homeless with mental illnesses, and black men probably make up the bulk of the homeless population. Both these estimates—that a high percentage of the homeless suffer from mental illnesses and that African American men make up a majority of the homeless in this country—are debated. They don't fit the image some advocates of the homeless want to project. They concentrate on the women and children who they say are the fastest-growing segments of America's homeless: women and children are more sympathetic subjects and it's a lot easier to lobby on their behalf.

Accurate counts of the homeless are hard to come by. Communities across the country each have multiple estimates that vary wildly. In Atlanta, for example, the homeless population may be anywhere from 3,000 to 40,000, depending on whose count is accepted. But however nebulous the numbers, no realistic attempt to address homelessness can ignore the major role mental illness plays in the problem. It is no coincidence that the explosion in the number of people living on our streets began with the phasing out of mental hospitals that started in the 1960s. That's when advances in treatment, which should have benefited all patients, were perversely twisted into a rationale for public policies that hurt the most vulnerable patients. With more effective medication and counseling, people with mental illnesses could lead more independent lives. An adequate support system would have allowed them to function in their communities instead of being warehoused in mental institutions. Deinstitutionalization of the patients seemed the most obvious and humane step to take. The problem was that the other half of the promise wasn't kept. The community-based mental health services that were supposed to replace mental hospitals in the 1980s were never funded. People with mental illness were literally shown the door without the support system they so desperately needed.

Once the streets were flooded with former patients, inevitably there came a flow of men into the jails and prisons that make up the largest and fastest-growing component of the back-door mental health care system. The chain reaction relationship between mental illness, homelessness, and incarceration was demonstrated by a Justice Department study. It showed that inmates with mental illness were twice as likely to have been homeless before they were sent to prison as were inmates who did not suffer from mental illness.

The phenomenon is seen across the country. The Los Angeles County jail routinely is called the world's largest mental institution. As Dr. Linda A. Teplin, the director of the psycholegal studies program at Northwestern University, told *The New York Times* in mid-1999, "Jails have become the poor person's mental hospital." And a disproportionate number of those poor people are black men.

While the 2000 U.S. Census says African Americans make up only about 12 percent of the nation's male population, more than half the men in America's jails and prisons are black. Here, by the numbers, is a glimpse of how bad it is for the incarcerated with mental illness:

- According to a 1999 report by the Justice Department's Bureau of Justice Statistics, roughly 283,800 of the nearly 2 million people behind bars in this country suffer from severe mental illnesses. That's 16 percent of the men and women in our jails and prisons.
- In its 2003 report "Mentally Ill Mistreated in Prison," the international group Human Rights Watch says the rate of mental illness in U.S. prisons is three times higher than the rate for the nation's general population. The report also says there are three times as many mentally ill people in America's jails as in our mental hospitals.
- A report issued in 2002 by the National Commission on Correctional Health Care said that, on any given day, between 13.1 and 18.6 percent of inmates in state prisons suffer from major depression.

There would appear to be a streak of light in this ominous dark cloud. The Bureau of Justice Statistics report says the lowest rate of mental illness among prisoners is the 13.5 percent for African American men. But this is without a doubt a false silver lining. The findings are based on interviews with prisoners, who were asked to self-report their mental illness. Of course, not only are black men less likely than whites to acknowledge their mental illness because of stigma; they also are less likely to have seen a therapist and received a diagnosis. From the juvenile justice system through adult prisons, behavior that might indicate a mental disorder is more likely, for blacks, to be ascribed to acting out.

Consider, for example, what happened when the boxer Mike Tyson invoked mental disorders to explain the explosive rages that overtook him both inside the ring and out. Even though he was supported by doctors' opinions, Tyson was ridiculed as nothing more than a thug making excuses. Had Tyson produced oncologists who said he suffered from cancer, no one would have questioned it for a moment. But because he produced psychologists who said he suffered from mental disorders, there was skepticism galore.

A great deal of skepticism is expressed whenever anyone mixes the issues of mental health and criminal justice. For the general public, discussions of the mental health of criminal suspects, defendants, or prisons inmates are nothing more than attempts to let someone get away with something. There's this idea out there that all criminals have to do is claim to suffer from mental illness, and they go free. The reality, of course, is that insanity defenses are rarely raised and that when raised, they rarely succeed. And states are moving toward giving juries options when they decide the fate of a defendant claiming to be mentally ill. Some allow juries to find that the accused is insane, but still guilty of committing the crime. In those cases, the defendant can be locked away for years, during which he will supposedly receive mental health treatment that will render him safe to return to the community.

Prisoners may indeed be the only Americans with a guaranteed right to mental health care, but it's often a dubious right. Corrections officials seldom budget for such care out of the goodness of their hearts. They are forced to by court orders, and they often try to comply with those orders as cheaply as possible. That means emphasizing the most inexpensive drugs and minimizing individual therapy rather than providing the most effective treatments. (In fact, mental health therapy in prisons has gotten the most media attention in recent years when prison officials have been placed in the absurd position of treating a death row inmate's mental illness in order to make him fit for execution.) In some ways, then, walking through the mental health care back door is only marginally better than being left out in the cold.

■ ■ ■

Prisons are depressing places. I know, because I've been in a few—mostly as a journalist, and never as a prisoner. My brief visits have been more than enough to show me that no matter how modern or humane jails are, they are not intended to lift inmates' spirits. Our prisons are primarily punitive, not therapeutic, which is why we should not allow them to become poor people's mental hospitals.

One of the prisons I've visited is the Georgia Diagnostic and Classification Center. It happens to be located in Jackson, the town where I grew up. It also happens that one of my brothers, Fred, served as the warden there. His first job at the prison was as a counselor for the state labor department. Eventually he transferred into the corrections department and moved up the ranks. The Diagnostic and Classification Center is the prison that serves as the routing point for inmates entering the state system. Here, the prisoners are evaluated and a decision is made about which facility is most appropriate for them to serve their sentence. The prison at Jackson is also the home of Georgia's death row, the place where executions are carried out.

Given all that, there's a lot of stress for everyone at the prison, inmates and employees alike. Visiting is enough to get a sense of this. I remember being at the prison once when an inmate collapsed in the recreation yard during a softball game. He was wheeled through the prison on a gurney, headed to the ambulance that would take him to the local hospital. His chest was bare; his skin was as pale as the underbelly of a catfish. Later in the day I learned that he had died at the hospital. It made me wonder how the men in that community—because a prison is a community, after all—cope with a major source of stress like death, whether it comes randomly or is decreed by the state.

I'm not surprised, then, that my brother answered an emphatic yes when I asked whether mental health care is an important and growing concern for him as warden. "Especially since Central State [Georgia's largest mental hospital, which included treatment for the 'criminally insane'] closed," he said. "Some of the people who would have gone there are put in the [prison] system now."

The trend my brother has seen holds throughout Georgia's correctional system, according to Dr. Richard L. Elliott, a professor of psychiatry and medicine at Mercer University School of Medicine in Macon, Georgia. "Between 1991 and 2001, the number of inmates in Georgia's prisons with serious mental illnesses more than quadrupled, from 1,251 to nearly 6,000," Dr. Elliott wrote in an April 2002, op-ed piece for the *Atlanta Journal-Constitution*. He also noted that a 1998 survey of mental health services in Georgia's jails showed the majority of sheriffs believed that the number of people with mental illnesses in jail had increased dramatically, largely because community services were unavailable.

My brother Fred told me he wished his budget allowed him to add to his mental health staff of one full-time director and two part-time therapists. On any given day, their caseload consists of about 300 to 350 out of the 1,800 inmates at the prison. "We definitely could use more people if we had the money," he said. "Of course, it's not easy to find mental health professionals who are willing to work in a prison."

There is mental health screening as inmates come into the prison, but it's mostly a matter of self-reporting. Reliance on prisoners' willingness to admit their own mental illness probably explains part of the disparity in the racial makeup of the inmates who receive mental health care at the prison: While the prison population is about two-thirds African American, more than two-thirds of those under treatment are white. Some prisoners come in with previous mental health treatment noted in their records. "We take steps if a prisoner is acting strange on the cell block," Fred added. But there's no doubt about the importance of—in the words of Lucia Fletcher, the prison's deputy warden of care and treatment—"picking out the right guys" for inclusion in the prison's mental health program. Resources are limited. There probably isn't enough to provide help for all those who need it. Spending dollars on those who don't need help wastes money and makes the situation worse for the inmates who do need help with mental problems.

"Our first goal is diagnosis—to identify the legitimate mental health issue," Ms. Fletcher told me. "Then we come up with a treatment plan. We want to treat only the seriously mentally ill, because of the cost."

Depression is one of the most common diagnoses, along with schizophrenia. I asked whether black inmates are more likely to try to avoid being diagnosed because of the stigma attached to mental illness in the African American community.

Ms. Fletcher thought for a moment before answering. "That may be a factor," she finally said, "but I think there's a stigma in general, especially among men. The people we see are probably the last ones in the world who would voluntarily get treatment."

The disparity between the percentage of black men in the prison population and the percentage in the mental health program may have a more pragmatic explanation, she said. More of the African American prisoners have been through the system before and know that being assigned to the mental health program will lengthen their stay at the Jackson facility before they are sent to the prisons where they will serve their sentences. The "permanent" prison may be closer to home and easier for families to visit, so most inmates want to get there as quickly as possible.

Do most prisoners arrive with mental health problems, or do most of them develop emotional disorders as a result of incarceration? I asked.

"We see it both ways," she replied. "We've never broken it down."

Are the ones who receive treatment—for whatever reason—better off for it?

"For the large majority, yes," Ms. Fletcher replied. "They're better off. Absolutely. We see a lot of guys who, once we get them stable on their medication, they become easier to work with and more compliant."

But what about helping them adapt to life outside prison? Does getting mental health treatment while inside make them less likely to return to prison after their release?

Lucia Fletcher paused, and though again. Then she said she's seen no information showing that mental health treatment in prison lowers the recidivism rate. But she mentioned a pilot program in Georgia that includes directing discharged inmates to mental health services in their communities. The early results show that former inmates who entered that program have a better chance of steering clear of trouble. There's a proposal in Congress that would take this approach nationwide. The Mentally Ill Offender Treatment and Crime Reduction Act, passed by the U.S. Senate in October 2003, provides for federal grants to establish more programs that seek to reduce recidivism among mentally ill offenders by helping them find mental health care once they are released. The legislation also authorizes federal funds to improve treatment for mentally ill offenders at all levels of the nation's criminal justice system.

Fred told me that the share of the prison's budget devoted to mental health care has increased in recent years. However he has to trim his overall budget because of across-the-board cuts being made throughout state government in Georgia. Most states face the same kind of fiscal crunch brought on by a combination of declining tax revenues due to the weak economy and a drying up of grants from an increasingly tightfisted federal government. A survey by the National Association of Governors found that more than thirty of the fifty states expected to face budget deficits in 2003. When the ax begins to fall on government spending, the budget items with the most vocal constituencies are the most likely to survive. Unfortunately, few voices are raised in support of mental health care for prisoners, and for that there's a price to be paid.

Robert Martin is a young black man who has been paying the price for much of his life. He began having serious behavior problems when he was in elementary school. His mother, Vernell Garrett, tried to find help for him, but there wasn't much help to be found. (I'll tell the full story of Vernell Garrett's perseverance later.) Teachers, counselors, and the police wrote Robert off as another bad black kid out of control. He wound up in the juvenile justice system and seemed to be headed for adult prison unless something changed. Something did change when a juvenile court judge sent him for a psychological evaluation instead of straight to a juvenile detention center. Robert was diagnosed with mood disorders, including depression. He was prescribed medicines that helped him control his outbursts.

But they only worked when he took them. When I met Robert he was nineteen years old and in jail. He had been arrested on a domestic abuse charge after a fight with his girlfriend. "She threw a pillow at me and I got mad," he said. "I lose my temper a lot, but when I do

I don't hurt anybody but myself. I punched a hole in the wall. I broke my hand doing it."

Robert told me he's able to control himself when he takes his medication. "But I have problems when I don't take it," he said. "I especially have trouble with authority." Despite this, he said, he preferred not taking the medicines because of the side effects. He also believes—as most people believe—that he ought to be able to control himself without relying on drugs.

He had been in jail several times. If he didn't mention his mental health problems when he was there, nobody asked about them. So when Robert was a child who didn't realize he needed help, the school and social services systems let him fall through the cracks. Now that he is an adult who resists the help that's available, the criminal justice system makes it easy for him to crawl through the cracks. In either case, no one's interest is served—neither Robert's, nor that of the people around him.

███

I've written quite a bit for newspapers about homelessness. Intractable problems tend to attract passionate people, and those who become activists and advocates on behalf of the homeless definitely are passionate. I've met some who are blinded by their passion. They treat homelessness as a right, rather than a problem. They expend more energy making sure the homeless are allowed to squat in abandoned buildings or camp in public parks than they expend helping the homeless find safe and sanitary shelter and lead independent lives.

But I've met at least one person who is both passionate and clearheaded about the homeless. He's Alan Harris.

Harris is a trim, soft-spoken man who has spent almost twenty years working on behalf of the homeless. He doesn't romanticize their plight as if it were a rugged lifestyle choice. And he doesn't shy away from the fact that serious mental illness would keep many of the homeless on the streets even if housing were made available to everyone who needs it.

"What we want to do is focus on the underlying causes of homelessness, which are, without doubt, addiction and mental illness," says Harris, who is a founder of Atlanta's Coalition for the Homeless Mentally Ill. "The system puts too many demands on people who are mentally ill and have no friends or family to support them."

On the basis of his own observations, Harris says that about one third of Atlanta's homeless suffer from serious mental illness. Some local advocates vehemently dispute that figure, saying that the rate of mental illness among the city's homeless isn't significantly higher than the 15 percent generally accepted for the national population. However, a 1997 survey by Research Atlanta, an independent think tank, found that 27 percent of the metro area's homeless suffered from serious mental illness. That's a significant rate, and it's not too far from Alan Harris's guesstimate.

I spent some time with Harris at Alpha House, a gathering place for the homeless men whom he and his wife, Nancy, help. The Harrises are white, but almost all of the men I met at Alpha house were black. I got to know one man whose story Harris said was fairly typical of the homeless men he encounters. I'll call him Jerry, because he didn't want his real name used.

Jerry told me he once had a family and a good job, but lost it all in a downward spiral into drinking and drug abuse. He wound up on the streets in Atlanta. He spent a lot of his time being hassled by the police or fighting with other homeless men over places to panhandle or to sleep. He hated going into shelters: It was like giving up his last measure of control over his life.

He eventually found his way to Alan Harris, who helped him get Social Security benefits and a mental health evaluation. He was diagnosed with several disorders, including clinical depression. The medications that were prescribed definitely helped, but he had trouble staying on them. He began a cycle of becoming stable enough to get off the streets into an apartment, only to stop taking his medication and wind up back on the streets.

I took notes as Jerry's words tumbled out at an ever more rapid pace. Suddenly he stopped. "You're writing down my life," he said with obvious agitation. "You can't do that. You can't just steal my story. I know what you're doing!"

"Calm down, Jerry," Alan Harris said. His voice was gentle and soft. "Nobody's trying to steal your story. We're going to go into the kitchen. If you're calmed down after a few minutes, we can talk again."

But Jerry didn't calm down. He stormed out without another word to me.

Harris told me the outburst was an example of the worst of Jerry's behavior when he doesn't take his medication. The system that allows men like Jerry to fall through the cracks is what worries Alan Harris. He has helped too many men get into shelters or into their own housing only to see them back on the streets because the follow-up help they needed simply wasn't there. The cycle starts again. The homeless with mental illness get attention only when they fall afoul of the law. It's not just that we allow them to become dangerous. It's that we look away and allow them to suffer.

* * *

Alan Harris is one of the volunteers who are part of the patchwork social safety net for people with nowhere else to turn for mental health services. The portion of the safety net that is the result of public policy involves places such as Atlanta's Grady Memorial Hospital and people like Dr. Keith Wood.

Dr. Wood is the director of the psychiatric center at Grady, Georgia's largest public hospital and one of the leading facilities of its kind in the United States. Public hospitals are supposed to be the places that can't turn you away when you really need help. They constitute a dying breed, as the government funding that sustained them for generations dries up and they are forced to compete in the marketplace dominated by for-profit hospitals. It's not a level playing field. The ideal patients for making a profit in medicine are the ones with the most money and the fewest, least serious health problems. Public hospitals attract patients with the least money and the most serious health problems.

Mental health care in hospitals has been especially hard hit. The number of hospital beds dedicated to patients with mental illness has declined across the nation in recent years. While it is true that mental health care advances allow more people to be effectively treated on an outpatient basis, that's not the only reason psychiatric beds are disappearing. The poor are more likely to use them, so they're not big moneymakers. As a result, inpatient services have been cut to the point that there is a widening gap between the care that's needed and the care that's available. This situation has a disproportionate impact on African Americans in general, because we tend to use inpatient mental health services rather than outpatient services. As former Surgeon General David Satcher told me, "African American patients are fifty percent less likely to seek outpatient mental health care than white patients."

Dr. Serravezza, my psychiatrist, served her residency at Grady, worked there part-time once she was out of medical school, and eventually volunteered to supervise psychiatric residents. She says things were very different there fifteen years or so ago: "What was nice back then was that when people needed to be in hospitals we actually had hospitals we could send them to. We had inpatient space. We had two wards for inpatients. We had a milieu [a ward that offered patients communal living], a stabilization unit, and an emergency room. We could actually take care of people and see them. We admitted them at night in the emergency room and could see them in the unit during the day. We actually got to know people, to follow people, get to know people over the course of several years, actually. A lot of people these days come in a state of crisis, are stabilized, and go home, which is a problem in a way. It's also got to be addressed."

The situation creates contradictory priorities for psychologists like Keith Wood. He wants adequate funding so that psychiatric beds will be there when they're needed, especially if the patients can't afford to pay for them. But he also says more resources should be devoted to the front end of the mental health care system. "Clearly, it's both more cost effective and we have better outcomes when we get people into treatment before their illness is acute," Dr. Wood told me. "Too many of the patients we see don't come in until they've reached a crisis point." Sometimes, Dr. Wood added, patients come into Grady's emergency room for treatment of an injury or illness, and doctors can see that they also need mental health care.

In addition to his duties at Grady, Dr. Wood has been active in efforts to bring mental health services to Atlanta's homeless, whether they are women and children in shelters or men living on the streets. "What's daunting about it," Wood said, "is that we have such a demand in terms of numbers."

* * *

Undoubtedly, there are those who would ask why it's important to worry about mental health care for these men on the margins—the poor, the prisoners, the homeless. As a practical matter, we might question the value of devoting limited resources to people who have so little to offer society, even when they've been at their best. Some might even question why I would lump these men together with the huge majority of African American men who are law-abiding and hardworking.

Alan Harris answers such questions by invoking God's injunction that we look after the needs of the least of his children. "It's an expression of my faith as a Christian and as a human being with compassion for other people," he says. "The only way I know to express my faith is to act it out."

For Dr. Keith Wood, the health care provider's obligation to ease suffering has nothing to do with the income or social status of those who suffer.

Those altruistic arguments alone would justify efforts to extend mental health screening and treatment to the men I've described in this chapter, especially when their illness is as common, identifiable, and treatable as clinical depression. But there are other reasons, less noble but just as important.

We must do something about mental illness among the homeless if we're going to make a dent in the problem of homelessness. Women and children may indeed be the fastest-growing segment of the homeless population. They definitely provide the problem with its most sympathetic face. But the hardcore homeless are men on the street—with black men making up the largest segment of that population—and mental illness is the reason many of them stay there.

As for our jails and prisons, their use as repositories for mentally ill men is misbegotten and expensive public policy. The 1999 Department of Justice study of incarceration of people with mental illness found that those who aren't treated remain behind bars longer and are more likely to return to jail once they're released. That's the worst kind of waste when you consider that the $20,000 to $30,000 most states pay to keep a man behind bars for a year is more than a year's tuition at some of our top colleges.

Finally, I have given deep and serious thought about how much of this book should be devoted to the problem of depression among African American men who are behind bars or living on the streets. And it did occur to me that taking up the cause of these men runs the risk of muddying the waters on the issue of getting help for the majority of black men who suffer from depression. Why reinforce the negative stereotypes of black men; why add to the stigma that's already attached to mental illness? And why give ammunition to those who will misinterpret this book as an attempt to excuse sins and failings of African American men?

Why? Because these men are our brothers, our fathers, our sons, our friends. We should treat them as we would want to be treated. And if we turn our backs on them, we hurt ourselves as much as we hurt them. If we let their illness run its course, their "contributions" to our community will be measured in hopelessness and despair. Instead of the assets we desperately need, they become reminders of our failure to act.

SIX

Is This Any Way to Treat a Black Man?

You don't know, you don't know my mind.
You see me laughin', laughin' just to keep from cryin'.

—Virginia Liston, Samuel Gray, and Clarence Williams,
"You Don't Know My Mind"

As the black middle class expands, as more black men land better jobs with more generous health benefits, the front door to mental health care opens wider for African American males. And while the heightened stigma of mental disorders has not been eliminated from the black community, progress is being made. The benefits of psychotherapy are more widely accepted. Increasingly, African American men have the means and the will to seek treatment for their depression.

But the barriers do not drop after we get through the front door. Mental health providers' ignorance of or insensitivity toward African American culture and a dearth of research on the special needs of black men undergoing psychotherapy combine to mean that a system designed to provide the most effective treatment available often fails to provide it to black men.

The trouble starts with the diagnosis. For example, a black male patient may present classic symptoms of clinical depression during his initial session with a nonblack therapist. But then the patient says the police are out to get him. Whenever he sees cops, he says, his anxiety level increases because he knows they will follow and stop him for no reason. And when he goes into a department store, the patient adds, security guards and salesclerks keep a close eye on him. He fears they will accuse him of shoplifting—again for no reason. After hearing this, the therapist veers away from a depression diagnosis and toward one of paranoid schizophrenia.

But for black men, anxiety about the police being out to get them and the feeling that they are being watched in department stores are not signs of paranoia. They constitute a recognition of reality. Police have been known to accost black men for no reason other than that they are black, and those incidents all too often result in the deaths of black men. Department store personnel sometimes do treat African American males more like potential thieves than prospective customers. Incidents such as these are not just in black men's heads; they are in the headlines.

The damage done by misdiagnosis or a misreading of the severity of a mental illness can be compounded when medication is prescribed. Carl Bell, who has published in medical journals on issues surrounding psychotherapy for black men, says he believes African American men too often are given antipsychotic medications when antidepressants are called for. This and other types of overmedication not only fail to treat the illness, they also unnecessarily subject patients to severe side effects that discourage them from taking *any* medications in the future, including the drugs that could help them.

Even a therapist who makes the right diagnosis and prescribes the right medication can fall short of providing effective treatment of depression in black men. Recent research—including work done by Dr. DiAnne Bradford at the Morehouse School of Medicine in Atlanta—has confirmed that a medication's effect can vary from one ethnic group to another. Dr. Bradford, who heads the clinical pharmacology section of the Clinical Research Center at Morehouse as well as the school's Minority Health Research Group, collaborated in work that pinpointed the characteristic that determines how the body processes medication. The findings showed a correlation between the characteristic and race.

"We took the first comprehensive look at the liver enzyme that metabolizes these drugs in African Americans," Dr. Bradford said.

Any physician knows that the effect of a medicine can vary from one person to another. Understanding that race may be a factor in how a person's body reacts would help a doctor determine which drug might be effective and in what dosage. For example, research by Dr. Bradford and others indicates that 30 to 35 percent of African Americans metabolize antidepressants at a slower rate than whites. (Other researchers put the percentage at up to 40 percent.) If the medicine is metabolized more slowly, a smaller dose will maintain the desired level of the medication in the bloodstream. And the side effects that result from a "standard" dose of the medication would be magnified in black patients.

"Our work shows that a cookie-cutter approach to prescribing medication isn't the most effective," Dr. Bradford told me. "It has implications ranging from which medications doctors should choose for their patients, to which ones health insurers should be willing to pay for."

The idea that a patient's race can be a factor in determining which medication a physician prescribes to treat an illness is controversial. It's repugnant to some. Even attempting to answer the question of whether medications can be more beneficial or more detrimental for one racial group than for others has generated resistance within the scientific community. An article titled "Racial Profiling in Medical Research" that appeared in the *New England Journal of Medicine* in May 2001 argued against "race-based medicine." For many doctors and researchers, injecting any racial consideration into the practice of medicine is the moral equivalent of bringing back the "White" and "Colored" doctors' waiting rooms of the segregated South.

Some of the cutting-edge scientific findings from efforts to assemble the intricately and infinitely complicated puzzle pieces that make up human beings argue against using race as any sort of criterion in the diagnosis and treatment of illness. The more we learn about our genetic makeup, the more the tendency to characterize ourselves based on skin color looks like folly. The Human Genome Project, after years of research into the basic building blocks of life, announced that the genetic code for human beings is 99.9 percent the same for everyone on the planet. This renders race meaningless, according to some scholars.

Yet we accept that a variation in even one gene can profoundly affect how that person's body functions, can determine which illnesses he or she is more likely to develop. We inherit our genes from our ancestors. People of different races have intermingled throughout history, but the tendency to stay within racial groups means the slight variation in genetic makeup is most likely to be handed down within those groups.

Of course, the researchers looking into how race might predict the effects of drugs on the body and the doctors who believe they can use the results of that research to improve the care of their patients don't argue that race should be the only consideration in prescribing medication. No one believes all people of the same race will have exactly the same reaction to a medication. At most, the research so far has shown that the percentage of people of one race who react to a drug in a certain way is different from the percentage of people of other races who react the same way. For example, there's the research showing that up to 40 percent of African Americans are slow metabolizer of antidepressants. On the basis on that information, no doctor would assume that all of his or her black patients should receive a lower than generally recommended dose of antidepressants.

But what doctor would fail to take into consideration that as many as 40 percent of his or her patients will react to the recommended dose of a drug differently from other patients? That would be significant in determining what dose to use at the beginning of treatment and in explaining why the medication doesn't work or causes unexpected side effects.

The question whether the race of a patient affects how a drug works shouldn't be beyond the bounds of scientific research. In fact, researchers should be conscious of the racial composition of the groups used to test the effectiveness of new medicines. The number of African Americans who participate in drug trials must increase, as

Dr. David Satcher strongly advocated during his tenure as surgeon general. The lack of black participation in clinical research is in part a lingering legacy of the distrust born out of the Tuskegee syphilis study. It's also part of the reality of a profit-driven drug industry, which concentrates on products that appeal to the largest and most affluent segments of the population. There's one thing those who decry "racial profiling in medical research" and those who see the benefits of such research should agree on: Anything resembling a "Whites Only" sign for drug trials must come down.

※ ※ ※

June Serravezza believes strongly in finding the medication that's best for individual patients. If a drug doesn't work as well as expected or causes side effects the patient is unwilling to tolerate, she tries an alternative. From the beginning of my treatment, she explained the options and possible side effects of various medications. We always had an open discussion, an exchange of ideas. She never simply said, "Take this."

We went through several antidepressants before we found one that was acceptable for me. Therefore, I can speak from personal experience regarding how a drug that has been thoroughly tested and proven effective still might not work for some people. I debated with myself whether in writing this book I should name the medications I've taken in the course of my treatment for depression. I was reluctant to do that because I feared I might create placebo effects for readers. If I write that a medication worked well for me, someone might take the same medicine expecting the same results and— voilà!—it works immediately. But it may only be the expectation created by reading about my positive experience that makes the medicine seem to work. If that's the case, the effect might not last.

Even worse, by naming medications that didn't work for me I might create a sort of reverse placebo effect for readers. If I detail my bad experiences with a drug, some readers might avoid it entirely or take each pill with a heavy dose of skepticism that I inspired. Staying on the medication would be made more difficult. This might happen even with a medication that could prove perfectly effective if given enough time to work.

Despite these concerns, someone convinced me that naming the medications makes this book a more complete and honest account of my experiences with my depression and my treatment for the disease. That being said, I strongly urge readers to remember that we all may react differently to medications. There will be a range of reactions within which most people will fall. But the range generally will be wide, and it must be taken into account that some people will have reactions that fall outside that wide range. Our low rate of participation in clinical trials that test the effectiveness and side effects of new medications makes it especially problematic for African Americans trying to figure out which therapeutic drugs will work best for us. I don't want black men or anyone else relying on me as a one-man clinical trial. You have to approach questions of which medications to take with an open and inquiring mind.

What's most important is having a therapist who knows what the medication options are and who listens to what the patient has to say about the effects he experiences. That's the kind of therapist I have in Dr. Serravezza. In fact, she gravitated toward psychiatry because of her medical school interest in the physiology of brain cell receptors and how a drug's effect on the receptors can affect mental illness. From the start of my treatment, she was willing to share her knowledge of medication with me in terms that I could understand.

Zoloft was the first antidepressant I took. According to Pfizer, the drug's manufacturer, Zoloft is the world's most prescribed antidepressant, with well over 100 million prescriptions having been written in the United States. It has proven to be perfectly effective for the huge majority of the people who take it. But my first dose of Zoloft made me violently ill. One pill sent me rushing into the bathroom to throw up like a commode huggin' drunk. It was an inauspicious introduction to the "wonder drugs" that were supposed to help lift me from the bottomless pit.

Dr. Serravezza didn't try to get me to hang in there—as in, "hang on to the toilet." She immediately switched to Plan B. Paxil was next up. My system tolerated it. However, I did notice that it seemed to cause slight vision problems, along with hand tremors and other motor problems serious enough to affect my ability to play tennis. (I should note here that I'm the type of tennis player who's always looking for a reason why I don't play as well as I think I should. I switch tennis racquets more often than most people switch toothbrushes. So, my sense that the side effects of a medication interfered with my tennis game should be viewed with great skepticism. In other words, the fault was probably not in my antidepressant; the fault was in my serve.) Dr. Serravezza told me it would be okay to take a weekend "medication vacation" once in a while to allow side effects to subside so I could more fully enjoy tennis and other affected activities. This is a step that shouldn't be taken lightly or without your doctor's knowledge. It works fine with some medicines, but with some others it can be harmful to stop taking the medication, even for a couple of days.

The search for a medication with minimal side effects led to Wellbutrin. A few days after I started taking it, I told Dr. Serravezza that I already was feeling less depressed. I definitely was doing better, I thought. She told me that probably was true—that I was "doing better" since helping me feel less depressed was what the treatment was all about. But she explained that the medication might not be the only thing making me feel better. Usually, it would take several weeks, at least, before the chemicals from the medicine accumulated in my brain at levels high enough to affect my mood. Dr. Serravezza said my expectation that taking the medication would make be feel better, along with the benefit of finally talking to someone about my depression, also played parts in improving my mood.

However, she also explained that medication can have immediate effects that are true indicators of things to come: "If you have initial *dramatically* negative response, you're probably on the wrong neurotransmitter path. Conversely, if there is an initial feeling of well-being, for whatever reason, you're probably on a better path. If nothing else, you can tolerate medicines for long enough to see if they can be helpful long-term."

I don't know if I'm a slow metabolizer of antidepressants that some research says many African Americans are. But I can see that people who have the trait may have problems at both ends of the antidepressant drug regimen.

First, the lag between when the patient begins taking the medication and when it begins to have an effect may be longer than average. This can be discouraging for those who don't get the possible placebo effect I got because I believed the medication would work. The longer it takes before the patient starts seeing some benefit from taking the medicine, the more likely he is to stop taking it.

At the other end of the process, being a slow metabolizer can make someone who goes off his medication more likely to stay off it. If we retain the antidepressant in our bloodstream longer, then we will feel the effects of the medication for a longer time after we stop taking it. Many patients stop taking their medicine because they feel better. This mistaken belief that medication has become unnecessary could be sustained longer by the slow metabolizer, lulling him into a false sense of security and making the return to medication more difficult. To top it all off, the slow metabolizer who goes back on an antidepressant would have a longer wait before the benefits return. Such a cycle of lose-lose situations would make it difficult for anyone to comply with a medication protocol.

Slow metabolizers' heightened adverse reactions to antidepressants create another major obstacle to taking the drugs as required. Side effects are one of the primary reasons why patients give up on medication. They have to weigh how much the drug enhances their enjoyment of life against how much it detracts from it. All too often it's easier to see the negative effects than the positive.

My discussions with Dr. Serravezza about how the Wellbutrin was working for me led to some fine-tuning. The medication's effects were generally good, but they could be uneven. I would have a definite down period most days. Changing the dosage didn't help. Dr. Serravezza decided I should try an updated version of Wellbutrin, formulated to release its active ingredients into the bloodstream slowly instead of all at once. In addition to spreading the benefits of the medication more evenly over the course of a day, it also makes differences in metabolism less important in determining whether the medicine is effective and at what doses. So sustained-release medications would be especially beneficial for slow metabolizers.

The balancing act that's required to give antidepressants the best chance of working can't be pulled off alone. There has to be a partnership between patient and practitioner. They have to be on the same page, even though what they want from a medication may sometimes be contradictory or even mutually exclusive.

As I've said, Dr. Serravezza has always been good about prescribing the medication that works best for me. Yet the only thing approaching a discordant note I can recall from our sessions over six years involved medication. It was a small but telling divergence of opinion about what made a medicine acceptable.

Sexual side effects, from dampened desire to an inability to reach orgasm, are among those most commonly experienced by people taking antidepressants. I noticed that one of the medicines I tried early on lowered my libido more than even the coldest shower could. I swallowed my embarrassment and worked up the courage to tell Dr. Serravezza.

Her response was not unsympathetic, but she essentially said there were more important considerations than my sexual urges, especially since at the time Claire and I were separated and it was unclear whether the marriage would survive. We certainly could look for a medication that wouldn't dampen my sex drive, she told me, but the first order of business was to find one that would help me move from a state of emotional crisis to emotional stability as quickly as possible. Under the circumstances, putting my sex life on hold should be no big deal.

And I thought: That's easy for you to say.

The sexual side effect of the medication was important to me. My dismay wasn't only about interference with my ability to have sex; it was about the loss of sexuality. I was less interested in things sexual.

The medicine was taking a pleasurable part of my life away from me. The feeling of loss was so strong that it evoked a physical sensation: I felt a lightness in my loins. This wasn't a matter of diminished manhood. I felt that the asexual being the medication was turning me into was more insubstantial and less of the flesh, less human than I wanted to be. My sexuality was a part of my identity that I was not going to give up.

Loss of sexual desire is one symptom of depression, and sexual dysfunction can trigger depression in men. But my depression hadn't affected my sex drive, even when I was at my lowest. So there certainly was an irony in my experiencing sexual side effects from a medication intended to treat my depression.

Dr. Serravezza was right, of course. I did have more important things to worry about, such as being suicidal, for example. No responsible physician treating a patient for clinical depression would collude with the patient by placing sex ahead of survival. The same would apply to other side effects: That balancing act has to take place.

I think most men would be concerned about the sexual side effects of antidepressants. Perhaps I was particularly sensitive about them it because I grew up in a culture where—for good or bad—the sexual component of manhood is emphasized. Fortunately, once my condition stabilized, Dr. Serravezza and I found that Wellbutrin effectively treated my depression with minimal sexual side effects. In fact, for many patients, Wellbutrin is the antidepressant that helps them reclaim their enjoyment of sex.

Any patient and therapist should have frank discussions about the sexual side effects of antidepressants. I imagine such discussions would be difficult for many men, and particularly difficult for many African American men. The subject is charged for us because of the stereotype of the black male as a "sexual animal." So, for some black men any embarrassment that makes them reluctant to raise the issue may be compounded by the fear that doing so confirms the stereotype. In truth, few people of any race would be unconcerned about the loss of sexual desire.

Issues surrounding medication are a potential mine field in the relationship between patient and therapist. I think this can be especially true when the patient is an African American man being treated for depression. We are less likely to seek help in the first place. We are more likely to be dubious about being dependent on drugs to help us do well emotionally; in fact, we grow up being told—and in too many cases learning from the experiences of people around us— that dependence on drugs is a bad thing. The mines in the mine field are even more explosive if the African American man is a slow metabolizer of antidepressants. It can take longer for him to feel the medicine's beneficial effects, giving any doubts he has more time to grow. Side effects are magnified, providing another reason for not taking the medication.

Dr. Serravezza deserves credit for our ability to safely negotiate the medication mine field. At the beginning of my treatment, I knew next to nothing about the antidepressants that were available. My role in this important element of my therapy was to tell Dr. Serravezza how I felt after taking each medication and what side effects I experienced. Things went well because she listened to me and was willing to try medications that addressed my needs, not simply medications said to work best on clinical study groups— groups that most likely included very few, if any, people like me.

The best advice I can give to an African American man being treated with antidepressants is this: Make sure your medication is prescribed by a health care practitioner whom you trust to make decisions based on your needs and who in return trusts your ability to determine and articulate those needs.

▧ ▧ ▧

Some psychotherapists—with African Americans in the field leading the way—argue that treatment of depression and other mental illnesses is more effective if based on patients' ethnic and cultural backgrounds. The American Psychological Association and the American Psychiatric Association have taken no official positions on whether treatment is more effective if the patient and therapist are the same race. However, the psychological association has published guidelines stressing that it is important for therapists to understand and be sensitive to the cultures of patients. And the psychiatric association is on record as supporting both increases in the number of minority therapists and the inclusion of cultural sensitivity courses in the training of therapists, a step a growing number of university programs are taking.

Such efforts to prepare mental health practitioners to treat patients from diverse backgrounds have been widely welcomed, but some of those who have been most active on this issue feel much more needs to be done. For example, Dr. Michelle Clark is a strong advocate of offering such specialized psychotherapists. The Special Emphasis Treatment Units she runs at the University of San Francisco provide a model: Factors such as a patient's race, gender, national origin, and sexual orientation are considered in structuring the course of treatment.

Dr. Clark maintains that treatment involving a patient and a therapist of different races or cultures is "very challenging, and that's putting the positive spin on it." She said a patient gives clues through language, by demeanor, and in other ways that are more likely to be misinterpreted by a doctor of a different race.

The issue is more than theoretical for Richard Mouzon, the African American psychologist in Atlanta whom I mentioned earlier. Dr. Mouzon himself has been in therapy for depression. He says he went through four white therapists and felt he was making no progress. While he respected all of them, Dr. Mouzon couldn't connect with those doctors in the way he believes is essential to successful treatment. It wasn't until he started working with a black therapist that he saw results.

"[African Americans] were really raised not to trust the white man, not to trust him with everything about us," he says. "When you've got to give up to a therapist your core issues, that's hard to do. It's almost impossible [for a black patient] to do with a white therapist."

The idea of "race matching" mental health practitioners with patients is, of course, a controversial one. It's racism to some experts, even some who are firm believers in considering patients' race in making a diagnosis and deciding on a course of treatment.

Dr. Peery Grant, a past president of the Atlanta Foundation for Psychoanalysis and a supervising analyst on the faculty of the Emory University School of Medicine, says the idea of matching patient and therapist based solely on race sounds like a racist notion once widely held in the psychoanalytic community—that a white therapist could not analyze a black patient, and a black therapist could not analyze a white patient.

"At the time I was being taught that, there were some very outspoken people at Columbia University who were fighting against that," Dr. Grant says. "They were able to . . . demonstrate that it wasn't true. It really was a prejudicial idea that was wrong."

Dr. Grant believes a therapist and patient of different races have an obvious obstacle to overcome, but it's not "a massive one. It's there, but it can be dealt with, is my point."

Quentin Ted Smith of the Morehouse School of Medicine came down somewhere in the middle on this issue. "There is some information out that sometimes people that have similar cultural and racial backgrounds seem to match up better as far as therapy is concerned," he told me. "But, at least in my experience, if you have a therapist from the same culture—let's say you're black and looking for a black therapist or you're white and you're looking for a white therapist—the match-up in race or culture does not guarantee that the therapist is going to be understanding and empathetic. They may be of the same racial background and the same culture, but their experience may be quite different from yours, and it may be difficult for them to understand your life experiences."

Carl Bell broke it down bluntly: "A bad white therapist is a bad therapist; a bad black therapist is a bad therapist."

※ ※ ※

Dr. Serravezza and I come from different backgrounds. The most obvious difference is that she is a white woman and I am a black man. We do share the experience of growing up in small Southern towns—she in North Carolina and I in Georgia—but otherwise our life experiences probably are quite different. Yet we have a patient-doctor relationship that worked from the start. I felt comfortable with her. She showed concern for me. I sensed genuine empathy.

I asked Dr. Serravezza about her early impressions of whether we would be compatible as doctor and patient. "You were very clear in describing to me what you were experiencing and what the issues were," she responded. "I had no sense of not being able to understand what was going on. If there had been a racial, cultural, or whatever kind of mismatch where it would have felt uncomfortable, I might have thought, 'Where's this guy coming from?' I didn't feel any of that. I try to bring a sense of neutrality into my first meeting with a patient so I can make an evaluation about treatment. With you, my neutrality then led to a feeling of 'I can understand this. I can deal with this. *We* can deal with this.' And that really didn't get shaken anywhere along the line."

Then she said something that, for me, was unexpected. "You had words," she said. "You had words to go along with the situation. You had a very eloquent narrative even in the very first session. As sad as you looked, the words that came out described your plight, and I understood how you felt." That assessment was unexpected because I remember feeling lost at sea during my first few sessions with Dr. Serravezza. I felt I was being battered by waves of emotions and I was struggling to express how I felt. But I was trying. I was talking. Dr. Serravezza deserves some credit for that. And she deserves a lot of credit for listening to me better than I was listening to myself.

That a black male patient could so quickly develop a rapport with a white female therapist would seem to fly in the face of the theory that mental health patients are better off being treated by someone who is like themselves. But I didn't say everything was perfect between Dr. Serravezza and me. There were moments when cultural differences arose—not necessarily as barriers, but as bumps in the road. There was, for example, the issue of my father.

I told her the story of my nonrelationship with my father—how he left the family when I was about four years old and how I could only remember seeing him two times in my life after that. I also told her I didn't feel deprived in any way, I didn't miss my father, and I certainly didn't feel any anger toward him any more than I would feel anger toward any other complete stranger, which was what he was to me. My father was so completely out of my life, I told Dr. Serravezza, that I didn't go to his funeral when he died.

She seemed to think this was extraordinary, that I must be harboring emotions about my father below the surface, perhaps at a depth I did not want to plumb. She returned to the subject a few times, especially when I talked about my relationship with my sons and how I knew I would be a part of their lives no matter what. I had a feeling that Dr. Serravezza was looking for a significance I refused to admit.

But there was none. For me, my father's absence was an unfortunate but not unheard of life experience. Two-parent households were the rule in the black community where I grew up, but there also were families where mothers were raising their children alone, as my mother did. We were not stigmatized or singled out in any way that I can recall. For most of us, the absence of a father didn't make us feel deprived, because our mothers refused to let us be deprived. In fact, we felt lucky compared to children whose fathers remained in the home only to heap abuse on them and their mothers.

Yet I knew deep down that my father was a presence in my life even by his absence. It's like being haunted by the idea of a ghost instead of by a ghost. The former is as frightening as the latter. This was something I didn't talk about. Even when I was most open with Dr. Serravezza, I didn't tell her about the episode that is emblematic of how my father affected me.

It happened when I was in college. I bought a lemon of a used car. It was about as reliable as . . . well, as a used-car salesman's word. I spent more time pushing it than I did driving it. It left me stranded on the interstate when I was driving down to see my mom one weekend. When I called to let her know what had happened, she surprised me: "You know your daddy is a mechanic," she said. "He's got a shop over on the Southside. I'll call him and ask him if he'll fix it."

I was shocked, because my mother hadn't mentioned my father to me in years. I had no idea she knew where he was, much less how to contact him. I hadn't seen him since I was a small child. The last time I could remember seeing him was in a courtroom, where a judge lectured and threatened him about his failure to make child support payments. In this memory he was not a person, just a vague figure with downcast eyes.

A few days later, Mom called me and said she had arranged for my father to get the car towed to his shop in Atlanta's Southside. He wanted me to come over so he could show me the work that needed to be done; he would call to set up a meeting. When the call came, the voice was mine, only with the country accent undiluted. He would pick me up the following Saturday. I gave him directions to the campus and said I would meet him on a corner near my dorm.

Saturday came and I was on the corner at the appointed hour. There was no sign of my father. I waited. After about half an hour, I went back to the dorm and stood by the pay phone for a while. It didn't ring. I was about to go back to the corner again when I realized something: I had no idea what my father looked like. He could drive by, and I wouldn't recognize him. I had no reason to believe he would recognize me.

I had this image of myself standing on the street corner, stopping passing strangers and asking, "Are you my father?" I didn't go back to the corner.

And I didn't tell my therapist that story.

So for an instant I felt there was a something of a cultural divide between Dr. Serravezza and me on the issue of my attitude toward my absent father. Yet the difference could be an asset instead of an impediment if we were willing to bridge the gap. Through my discussions with her I saw the significance of my feelings about my father, and I understood that I had developed an ability to minimize that significance in my own mind. Perhaps this is an imperfect but important coping device I and other African American men use to deal with a fundamental trauma in our lives: the absence of a father.

I asked Dr. Serravezza whether this kind of learning flows both ways between a doctor and patient, and whether she thought it happened that way with us.

She answered yes on both counts.

"There was a lot that you revealed to me that perhaps I didn't have an understanding of, but you were able to clarify so that I could understand," she said. "Your father, for instance. You explained that, and I could understand in a certain kind of way. You gave me a clear understanding of how you wanted to be involved in your sons' lives. That was very poignant to me. You taught me a lot in that regard, but there wasn't anything foreign about it, or strange. I think it's a good match."

The question of how much race matters in the relationship between therapist and patient is double-edged in other ways, of course. If there are barriers that make it difficult for a white practitioner to effectively treat a black patient, similar barriers must stand between a black practitioner and a white patient. That's bad news for the relatively small number of minority therapists. Such thinking cuts them off from the largest segment of people who, in business terms, make up their market.

Dr. Mouzon, who treats whites in his Atlanta practice, believes establishing trust can be easier for a white patient seeing a black therapist than it is when the situation is reversed. "That's because whites tend to see blacks as nurturers," he says, referring to the traditional roles of African Americans as servants and caregivers. Even in the segregated South, of course, the sight of blacks tending to white children and the elderly was common. The saying was that blacks were loved by very young white people and by very old ones; the years in between were the problem.

I found Dr. Serravezza more by chance than by design. There were no particular attributes or characteristics I was looking for in a therapist. In fact, I was so ignorant about depression that I thought I would have a couple of sessions with her, get a prescription for something to help me sleep through the night, and that would be that. I couldn't have been more wrong. Things had gotten so bad that I really had to have professional help, but I didn't understand how bad they were.

Perhaps if I had had a genuine appreciation for the condition I was in and the long process involved in dealing with it, I would have gone about the search for a therapist in a more methodical way. I might have gotten more recommendations from which to make a choice. I probably would have spent more time interviewing candidates before deciding which one to see. If I had settled on a male African American therapist, the dynamics of the process probably would have been different in some ways.

Suppose Carl Bell had been my therapist. The first time I met him in person was at the Carter Center in November 2000. The recount of Florida's presidential ballots was under way. More details about what went wrong with Florida's voting were emerging. People at the Carter Center meeting were buzzing about butterfly ballots and hanging chads. Carl Bell's first words to me were about the story alleging that police set up traffic stops near polling places in black neighborhoods to discourage African Americans from voting, especially black men who might have had run-ins with the law. He seemed clairvoyant, because that was the thing that was most on my mind that day. But he wasn't a mind reader. We had life experiences that gave us a similar sense of what was truly outrageous yet plausible. Being simpatico in that way certainly would have been an asset over the course of therapy.

And when I've spoken to Dr. Sandra Walker, the African American psychoanalyst in Seattle, her ideas about the importance of confronting the legacy of slavery and the psychic trauma of racism resonate with me. I have no doubt about how much her insights could help me understand and cope with my depression.

But even as I recognize the benefits I would have gained from being treated by an African American therapist with the talents and sensitivity of Dr. Bell, Dr. Walker, or others I've talked to for this book, that doesn't diminish the results I've gotten with Dr. Serravezza.

This is what the Surgeon General's report "Mental Health: Culture, Race and Ethnicity" has to say: "When they use mental health services, some African Americans prefer therapists of the same race or ethnicity." But, as Carl Bell puts it, a good therapist is a good therapist.

SEVEN

Depression Is a Tough Row to Hoe

Sometimes I wonder, just what am I fighting for.
I win some battles, but I always lose the war.

—Doc Pomus and Mac Rebennack,
"There Must Be a Better World Somewhere"

Struggling with untreated clinical depression means living the most secret of secret lives. When you're in the tightening grip of the disease, it's a life you don't show to anyone else, no matter how close they are to you. You don't seek out others who are living the same kind of life; you're convinced that there *are* no others who suffer the way you do. The "suffering without meaning" that the Holocaust survivor and psychiatrist Victor Frankl spoke of is the kind of misery depression can visit upon you.

You learn to hide what you come to see as the worst part of yourself. That's the part you inflict only on yourself. That's how you get by in the world. That's how you function. You learn to compensate in public. If your illness is bipolar, you don't have to learn to compensate. Compensation to the nth degree comes naturally when you're in a manic phase. That's the part of you that craves attention. To the world, it has the energized brilliance of a shooting star that blazes across the night sky. To you, your manic self is a flare shot off from the darkness of depression.

Most of the people around you—even those closest to you—are

made unwitting accomplices in the conspiracy of silence that hides your illness. The idea that you or anyone else they know might be suffering from depression is foreign to most of them. Even those who understand that depression can strike anyone are reluctant to apply the label to you or to anyone else. Within that small circle of people who recognize your depression for the serious problem that it is, there are a select few, if any, who can put aside their own embarrassment—or their fear of embarrassing you—long enough to talk to you and advise you to get help.

If any depression sufferers should consider themselves lucky, it is the ones who have people in their lives willing to talk with them about their illness. But even those fortunate few are far from being home free. Having friends or loved ones or anyone else with the concern, compassion, and courage to confront you about your mental illness is less than half the battle. Your more difficult and important fight is with yourself. As painful as it is for the people around you to see the state you're in, they at least are salved to some degree by distance and objectivity. There are no such balms for your pain. Your depression is not only a part of you; it overwhelms all else that is you. You are wrapped in it. You are bound by it. All that you see of the internal and external worlds is filtered through the dimming lens of depression.

These are my impressions of what clinical depression is like in general. They are based on what I've learned through my experiences, from research, and also in talking with people who treat depression and who suffer from the illness themselves. Of course, no two cases of depression are exactly alike. The more we learn, the more we limit the list of causes of the disease of the brain we call clinical depression. But the paths to getting treatment for depression and the ways in which we respond to treatment once we get there are infinite. These factors are so dependent on who we are, and how we got to be who we are, that they are as varied as our individual personalities.

Still, some things link our lives and connect us within groups. Such common threads don't predict our behavior, but they are powerful influences on how we experience events in our lives, including depression. To meet the challenges presented by depression in African

American men—dealing with the public health implications of how the effects of the disease ripple through our communities, or with how it affects black men as individuals—we must understand what is distinctive about suffering from depression as an African American man. I don't have to rely on impressions of what that's like. Doing research and talking to experts has taught me a lot about depression and black men. But most of what I know about the subject has come from my own experience. I've learned about depression the way an avalanche survivor learns about snow.

Bits and pieces of my story appear throughout this book. I've used personal anecdotes when I've felt they bolster a point or when my experience supports or contradicts the scientific research on depression. But I want to use this chapter and the next to present a fuller account—my informal case history, if you will. I don't do so because I believe what I've gone through is particularly dramatic or heartwarming. And I certainly don't claim that my experiences are typical: I don't believe there is such a thing as a typical story of depression. There are as many distinctly different stories as there are people who suffer. What I hope is that readers will find my experiences instructive. I hope they are instructive for anyone affected by depression. But I hope they are especially instructive for African American men and for the people who care about them.

■ ■ ■

It all came crashing in on me the day of my emotional breakdown in early 1996 as I looked out the office window at the *Atlanta Journal-Constitution*. That one event told me how much in trouble I really was. For me, it was more frightening than the flirtation with suicide that initially convinced me to get help. The breakdown was an assault on my idea of who I was and what it meant to be a man. I had kept my emotions under wraps for virtually my entire life. The cracks in the dam—when there were cracks—almost always appeared in private. There were no witnesses to the emotional seepage, the flow of tears. But that day, suddenly, I not only lost control of my emotions, I was unable to keep my emotions out of public view. That, to me, was the ultimate humiliation. Living that way seemed a worse fate than taking my own life.

I knew then that something was desperately wrong. Knowing is one thing; understanding is another. My inclination always has been to try to understand. Knowing what was happening to me—that I was suffering from clinical depression—wasn't enough. I wanted to understand this thing that was happening to me. Understanding meant getting beyond the what to the how and the why.

Eventually, I decided that the understanding I sought lay at the intersection of two paths. One path involved reconstructing my depression; the other path involved deconstructing my life. Along the former, I would find the causes—or building blocks—of my depression. Along the latter, I would find the reasons for how I react to and am affected by depression. I've trod these paths with varying vigor, thinking at different times that one was more important than the other if I wanted relief from my suffering. I started taking steps toward that imaginary intersection where understanding resides from the moment I began treatment for my depression. I didn't realize it at the time, however. I was overwhelmed by the mental state I had fallen into, and by the drastic measures I needed to take in order to climb back up.

"Do you think you'd do better if you were hospitalized?" Dr. Serravezza asked me near the end of the emergency session that followed my meltdown.

I was shocked by the question. I knew that hospitalization for depression wasn't routine. (I later learned that only about 5 to 10 percent of people who suffer from major depression spend any time in the hospital, and that most of them are hospitalized at a time when they are believed to be suicidal.) To me, it was significant that Dr. Serravezza would even ask the question. It meant she thought hospitalization was an option. Perhaps she was even leaning that way. Maybe by asking me whether I thought going into a mental hospital would help—by, in essence, making it my decision—she was softening the blow.

And it was a blow. It was a blow to my self-image and to the way

I wanted other people to see me. At that point in my life, I saw commitment to a mental hospital, even if it was voluntary, as an indication that a patient either couldn't take care of himself or was a danger to himself or to others. I had no doubt that most of the people I knew had the same view. My main worry was what those people would think of me. Surely, word would get out, especially at work. If you want to find a place where there are no secrets, where gossip travels faster than the speed of sound, try a newsroom. Just the idea that people would think of me as helpless—or, worse yet, dangerous—made me burn with shame.

This mistaken notion that mental illness is inextricably linked to violent behavior is one of the principal sources of fear and prejudice toward people with mental illness. This is especially true regarding black men, because of the way we grow up thinking about violence and the way society in general associates violence with us. There's a complicated dynamic at play concerning African American men and violence. The willingness to resort to force is both honored and abhorred as a trait of the black male. We grow up with the idea that a real man is someone you don't mess with. We're also taught that there are times when a black man is a fool to even think violent thoughts, no matter how much he is provoked. Being in the presence of a police officer is one such situation. We're most feared by people who are not like us, but we do the most damage to each other.

Even the idea that mental illness leads to violence is a two-sided coin among African American men. True, it's a source of the stigma against mental illness. But it's also an accepted survival strategy. Richard Pryor, Eddie Murphy, and Sinbad have all done comic riffs based on the kid who's a wimp, but tries to scare away bullies by "acting crazy." It's a joke, of course, but the reason it's a comedy staple and gets laughs is the spark of recognition it stirs in audiences.

But talking with Dr. Serravezza, I found nothing funny in the thought that people who heard that I had been in a mental hospital would automatically think of me as violent. The stereotype of the violent black male was enough of a burden. It was irritating enough to see people avert their gaze when I approached them on the street, or tense up if they happened to look over their shoulder to find me walking behind them. I didn't want the added baggage of seeing fear in coworkers' eyes because they heard I was the guy who got committed.

"No," I told Dr. Serravezza. "I don't think I need to be in the hospital."

Dr. Serravezza must have sensed some of what I was feeling. No doubt, the same reaction had registered on the faces of other patients. She explained that it wasn't just a matter of whether I *needed* to be in a hospital. The question was whether a hospital was the best place for me at the time. We had discussed whether I was suicidal. I honestly felt that I wasn't, and Dr. Serravezza seemed satisfied that I didn't intend to kill myself. She spoke about a mental hospital as more than a place where I would be safer; it was a place where I would be under less stress. I would be able to get some rest. A hospital stay of just a couple of nights might be the most effective way to get me stabilized.

Then she said something that made perfect sense: "If a doctor told you that you were suffering from exhaustion and said you needed to be hospitalized, you would go to the hospital, wouldn't you?"

"Yes, I would," I said. What Dr. Serravezza was doing, of course, was trying to get me to think of my mental illness as I would a "physical" illness. And the analogy to exhaustion was particularly apt. I really did feel I was suffering from "emotional exhaustion."

But I still thought hospitalization wasn't necessary. After more discussion, Dr. Serravezza agreed. We would keep the option open, however. I would monitor my mood over the next couple of days. If I felt there was further decline, I would contact Dr. Serravezza and we would again consider a hospital stay.

Meanwhile, there was the question of work. My idea was that I would take off a couple of days. I thought that would be enough time for me to get over my embarrassment. Once again, Dr. Serravezza had other ideas.

The timetable for my going back to work shouldn't be governed by how long it took me to get over my embarrassment. Everything depended on pulling me up from my depression, which might take a while. I had no more business being at work than a person with any other serious illness, Dr. Serravezza said.

Then she asked me a question I hadn't asked myself: "Are you capable of doing your job in the condition you're in right now?"

I had one of those moments in which you feel as if you're caving in on yourself. I could hear my heart pounding. "No," I said. "I don't think I am."

It was a difficult admission. I had spent more than twenty years using my writing skills to earn a living. The newspapers where I'd worked—the *Detroit Free Press,* the *Atlanta Journal-Constitution,* and *USA Today*—are high-profile publications, any one of which most journalists would be happy to have at the top of their résumé. Nonnewspaper work I'd gotten into print included short fiction, feature articles for magazines, and a book. Working as Mayor Maynard Jackson's press secretary and speechwriter was a plum political job. I had been a lecturer in journalism at my college alma mater. I had won awards for my writing. And the job I held at the time of my breakdown was the summit of years of climbing the journalism career ladder, starting as a cub reporter and reaching a position as an editorial board member and columnist.

Now, after accumulating all those accomplishments, I was telling someone that I no longer felt I was capable of doing my job. But, of course, I had a secret: For most of my working life, no matter how high I rose or how much positive reinforcement I received, I'd had doubts about my ability to do the job. There were times when my work brought me joy, but mostly it was a source of anxiety and self-recrimination. During the down times—and that meant most of the time—I believed my negative assessments of my abilities were realistic. Looking back now, I know that the ever darkening veil of depression was obscuring my view of myself. And I know that, as a black man, I carried an extra burden piled on as racism fed and compounded these feelings.

Despite my self-doubts, however, I did my job. More important to me, it had never been necessary to tell anyone explicitly about my negative self-evaluation; self-deprecating humor was the way I told people what I thought of myself without their realizing that I meant it. And I never flat-out told anyone that I couldn't do my job. But now, sitting in that quiet room, I had told someone just that.

And it was true: I wasn't doing my job. At that point, I was so deep in my depression that just about everything about work was too much for me. Even the most simple and basic things were difficult. Picking up the telephone to call someone required an effort. That meant people who left voicemail messages for me often didn't get callbacks, and calls I should have made to get information for my editorials either were not made or were put off until the last minute. I was barely making deadlines. I wasn't doing my best work.

Everything argued for my taking a leave of absence. Still, I felt guilty about doing so. I was letting down my colleagues on the *Constitution* editorial board, I thought: Their workload would increase while I was gone. To my mind, taking an extended leave would make me a traitor to a lot of people, including African American journalists past, present, and future. What kind of example would I set? Wouldn't I reinforce the stereotype of black men, the stereotype that says that mental toughness is not our forte?

Such thinking was silly on its face. Certainly, no one held me up as the standardbearer for black journalists. My success or failure had nothing to with the fortunes of any other employees at the *Journal-Constitution*. But that was the way my mind was working. I denigrated myself and placed blame on myself when there was no reason for blame. The power of positive thinking is no match for clinical depression.

I took the leave. I was gone for more than a month. I was fortunate to work for a company that would allow me to take that much time. My guess is that, in the vast majority of workplaces in this country, men would have a tough time convincing their bosses to give them any time off to deal with depression. They would face a choice between keeping their jobs and treating their depression effectively.

Still, despite my good fortune my path to treatment was the same in some important ways as it would be for most African American men. The most important similarity is the necessity to overcome barriers that keep us from treatment. My first barrier was ignorance of what depression is. Then came the shame and fear brought on by the realization that I needed help. As I said before, I know that a black man with depression has a tough row to hoe. I'm here to tell you that the row can be hoed, allowing a plant called hope to flourish.

■ ■ ■

What caused my depression?

I asked myself that question at the very start of my treatment. Just as most people would, I looked externally for the answer. I rounded up the usual suspects, major events that would make anyone sad: My marriage was failing. I was frustrated by my failure to be the kind of father my sons needed. Work had become a stressful grind most of the time. Looking at my life, I saw I wasn't living the life I'd once hoped to live.

But I was looking for answers in all the wrong places. Such events made me sad, but they were more likely to be *caused* by clinical depression than to be the cause of it. I should have been looking inward for the answer to my question, because the people who'd told me over the years that my depression was all in my head were right in ways they couldn't imagine.

Early on in my treatment, Dr. Serravezza explained the rudiments of the most widely held explanation for depression: Certain chemicals in the brains of people with clinical depression might be out of balance; antidepressants work by restoring that balance. But I wondered how these chemicals in my brain got out of balance in the first place. Researchers have given several answers to this question. Some believe we're hardwired at birth to have the chemical imbalance as our brains develop. Dr. Kay Redfield Jamison, who has written so eloquently about her own experiences with bipolar disorder, has collaborated in research that provides strong evidence of a genetic component in the predisposition toward manic-depression.

There also is considerable evidence that incidents involving physical or emotional trauma may cause clinical depression. (These should be distinguished from triggering events that send people who already have the illness into a downward spiral.) There's plenty of evidence that such traumas don't just change the way we feel emotionally; they also can change the way our brain works—perhaps even change its very structure. The converse of the theory also holds true: Some events or activities—such as exercise and meditation—change the brain, but with positive results. (Once, trying to impress on me the importance of exercise in promoting emotional health, Dr. Serravezza told me that a good workout was worth a dose of my antidepressant.) There is nothing that says that among these and other theories only one is right. They could all be right. There may be many causes of clinical depression.

I'm not qualified to choose among the theories and say which explains why I developed the disease. Medication definitely helped ease my depression, so I would say that chemical imbalance in the brain is a factor in my case. Like too many black men, I'm handicapped in trying to determine whether genetics are involved. To put it in scientific terms, I don't have the data. To put it plainly, I never got to know my father. He left our family when I was very young. His drinking is my clearest memory of him while he was in the home. As for his father—my paternal grandfather—I have no recollection of him at all; if I ever knew his name, I don't recall it now. I can say that my memory of my maternal grandfather, with whom I spent a lot of time, is of a quiet, brooding man.

As to whether the traumas I've experienced were causes of my bouts of depression, or merely triggering events, I don't know. For most of my life, I thought of myself as a person who was destined to be unhappy. There were times when traumatic events sent me into deep depression, but I also sometimes fell into funks for no apparent reason. However, I do believe that positive events and activities—talk therapy, for example—can alleviate clinical depression for the long term.

Finally, what about racism? Did it affect my depression? I can't see how it could not have.

I say that while setting aside the question of whether a given factor causes clinical depression or only adversely affects someone who is already clinically depressed. In both situations, mental health is affected—just as physical health is affected by microbes that weaken the immune system, after which other microbes attack the body. There is scientific proof that stress attacks human beings, weakening the body and making it vulnerable to a variety of diseases. Studies show that the stresses of poverty and racial discrimination are devastating African American in urban areas.

Helen Epstein highlighted this in an October 2003 article published in the *New York Times Magazine*. "Poor urban blacks have the worst health of any ethnic group in America, with the possible exception of Native Americans," Epstein noted in that piece, "Ghetto Miasma: Enough to Make You Sick?" Young African Americans in predominantly black big-city communities such as "Harlem, central Detroit, the South Side of Chicago and Watts have about the same probability of dying by age 45 as whites nationwide do by 65, and most of this premature death is due not to violence, but to illness." And the article also cited a study by the Harvard researcher Nancy Krieger showing that working-class blacks who accepted unfair treatment as a fact of life had higher blood pressure than those who resisted discrimination.

There's no doubt that stress can also be a factor in mental health problems, including depression. And there's no doubt that being poor can be stressful. These two facts were first scientifically linked when a 1963 study found that stresses brought on by poverty can lead to psychiatric disorders. That has been confirmed by subsequent studies, including one in 1994 that is the largest look at the mental health of Americans, involving a survey of 8,000 people. The study's lead author, Dr. Ronald Kessler of the Harvard School of Public Health, says he believes poverty-related stress causes this country's poor to have a rate of clinical depression that is two to three times higher than the average for the general population.

Helen Epstein's *Times Magazine* article reported that a U.S. Department of Housing and Urban Development (HUD) program to move residents of impoverished inner-city communities to better neighborhoods produced unexpected benefits. The people who moved enjoyed better health, including mental health. HUD researchers found that adults in New York who were moved by the program were less prone to depression and anxiety than those who stayed behind.

Being black—or being anyone else who is the target of racism— isn't the same as being poor. But dealing with racism is stressful. As I said early on in this book, some researchers believe that living under such stress can cause clinical depression. In their view, therefore, racism can cause African Americans to suffer from depression.

Again, from where I sit, whether racism is a cause or catalyst for my depression is academic. What I know as a black man is that racism affects how I fall into depression and it affects my ability to climb out. It does so because it affects the way I think about myself. Racism is psychological warfare in the most literal sense of the term. And, as has been true since human beings first organized themselves into armies to wage war, males are the primary targets.

It is no coincidence that Frantz Fanon, considered a founding father of the black consciousness movement of the early 1960s, studied and practiced psychiatry. His writings on colonialism, including the books *Black Skin, White Masks* and *The Wretched of the Earth*, explain racism as the means by which colonizers control the way the colonized think about themselves. Such mind control is essential to colonialism and to any other system in which one race subjugates another.

The system of segregation in which I grew up was not solely or even primarily about keeping the races separate. Despite the separate drinking fountains, bathrooms, schools, and the rest, there was plenty of interaction between the races. Segregation both explicitly and implicitly made clear which of those races was superior. Our separate but unequal facilities were intended to make us feel inferior, humiliated, and hopeless. If that's not a formula for depression, I don't know what is.

It's interesting to me how much the "black pride" movement

mounted to fight the effects of American racism has in common with the "talk therapies" used to fight clinical depression. In fact, the movement was like a decades-long mass psychoanalysis, using images such as Mother Africa, the return to the motherland, the replacement of self-hate with self-love, and the dream that Dr. Martin Luther King, Jr., said showed how we really wanted our lives to be. This was an attempt to make us change the way we thought about ourselves. It was not only a movement for equal rights; it was therapy.

I doubt I became clinically depressed or prone to depression solely because I've felt the sting of racism. As I've said, I've been fortunate in life. There are people who stood up under a burden of racial oppression a hundred times heavier than anything I've experienced. I would wager that most of them are not depressed. Some are the most optimistic people in the world. Yet I can't imagine that any of them would argue against the proposition that racism takes a toll on the emotional health of the people who are targeted.

The case for a racism-depression nexus—especially with regard to black men—is strengthened by research published in August 2003. A Virginia Commonwealth University study, led by the psychiatric geneticist Dr. Kenneth S. Kendler, who also directs VCU's Virginia Institute for Psychiatric and Behavioral Genetics, found that a person who suffers humiliation is at great risk for major depression. The VCU researchers interviewed more than 7,300 twins in an attempt to determine what life events trigger major depression and anxiety. This was the largest study of its kind, and the first to look at men as well as women. The results contradicted some of the most basic and longest-held beliefs about the causes of depression.

For many years, mental health practitioners thought major depression was most likely a reaction to loss, such as the death of a parent or other loved one. But the VCU study found that adding humiliation to the mix is the key to predicting which life events lead to major depression.

"When we looked at stressful life events that predisposed men and women to the onset of episodes of depression, the most toxic com-

bination was loss and humiliation that in some way directly devalu-
ated the individual in a core role," says Kendler.

A humiliating end to a romantic relationship—as when one person is dumped for someone else—was the event most often cited as
a catalyst for depression. But any humiliation that diminishes a person in his society could have the same effect. This is where racism
comes in, because racism at its core is about devaluing black people
through humiliation—especially the humiliation of black men.
Racism always has been and continues to be a systematic attempt to
devalue our manhood and to deny us social status in the most
humiliating ways possible.

Kendler says that having a humiliating loss of social status result
in depression makes sense in the scheme of human evolution. It's
easier to maintain order in a society if those who have been humiliated become depressed. That way they would withdraw from social
contact and use fewer of the community's basic resources such as
food, rather than reacting with rage against the individual who
caused the humiliation or against the society in general.

It's not difficult to imagine that the evolutionary basis for this
reaction to humiliation is specifically connected to the status of
males. In the fights for dominance within social groups of primitive
humans, defeated males relegated to lower social status no doubt felt
humiliation. If humiliation triggered depression, it was just as well,
since depression lowered the defeated males' desires for food, sex,
and other essentials to which the dominant male would claim first
rights.

Of course, we no longer live in primitive social groups ruled by an
alpha male who has fought his way to the top. We now believe that
subjecting people to humiliation is inhumane and wrong. But people still are humiliated in ways large and small. Racism serves African
American men humiliation in large doses. Thanks to the VCU study,
the scientific evidence for how racism can cause depression has been
strengthened.

Anecdotal evidence abounds. We all know African Americans
who feel ground down by racism. These are not always people who

fall prey to the feelings of powerlessness or hopelessness that racism is intended to instill; the range of reactions is more complex than that. For example, Gwendolyn Knight, the widow of the African American artist Jacob Lawrence, was interviewed in connection with an Atlanta exhibition of her husband's work. She was asked what impact racism had on his life. She said Lawrence suffered from depression, and she believed racism was in part to blame: Not only did racism make it more difficult for him to achieve success as an artist, it also denied him the full enjoyment of his success because he was wounded by the jealousy of black artists who were unable to overcome the barriers he overcame.

For any African American, the impact of racism is not limited to the effects on him or her as an individual; the harm it does to others also matters. That's one reason why even those who achieve the greatest triumphs over racism are not immune from its emotional damage. I see Dr. King as the embodiment of this. I know of no finding that he suffered from clinical depression (though someone in the FBI may have hoped he did, as evidenced by the agency's effort to pressure him into suicide with threats of revealing extramarital affairs). But the lack of a documented diagnosis notwithstanding, there is no doubt that Dr. King went through periods of deep despair. Historians of the civil rights movement, including Taylor Branch and David Garrow, have written about these lows in Dr. King's life. One sign of these funks was his talk of the intractability of racism. He spoke of his fear that it would always weigh black people down, and always contaminate the souls of white people. The idea that the FBI could push Dr. King to suicide is almost laughable. Yet during his emotional lows—especially near the end of his life— there were signs that his courage in the face of death transmuted into a death wish. In fact, that's how some have interpreted his "I've Been to the Mountain Top" speech on the eve of his assassination in Memphis. They see his refrain of "I may not get there with you" as more than Dr. King acknowledging his mortality. They see it as a worn-down Dr. King welcoming his mortality.

Getting past depression means dealing with the things that cause the illness to manifest itself. For African Americans, especially African American men, that includes dealing with the way racism affects us. This certainly has been necessary for me in my battle with depression, in my effort to move beyond knowing about the disease into understanding it. The influence of race in our culture has always been pervasive, yet so much of it remains unspoken today. We've made enormous progress toward eliminating the overt power of racism in our lives. But it still holds some sway over us in ways we don't even notice. That subtlety is what makes it so dangerous. It can color the way others see us and the way we see ourselves. Most often, the portrait that's painted is negative.

The black man who is successfully treated for clinical depression is not magically shielded from the impact of racism. He is not immune to its effects. However, he is better equipped to face the challenges racism presents in every aspect of his life. This is one of the peripheral benefits of getting help, yet it may be the most important. Race may not even come up during the treatment of depression. Still, a black man who deals with his depression will find that his ability to withstand and overcome racism will grow.

I've heard people talk about the allure of depression, about how it can be like an addictive drug. As painful and destructive as depression is, it has the appeal of numbing us to all else about life, be it good or bad. This is one way the disease perpetuates itself. It makes us fear getting better. Inaction becomes our default setting.

This is a dangerous state of mind for anyone, but it is especially dangerous for black men. It is a form of surrender we cannot afford. Embracing the fatalism of depression, we put ourselves at the mercy of a hostile world. Depression desensitizes us to the wrongs our people endure and leaves us incapable of doing the best we can do for those who depend on us for guidance, support, and protection. I had trouble seeing this and other realities until I had taken the first few steps into treatment. Before then, the decision to get help was a choice. It took a little while to realize that it actually was a necessity.

EIGHT

Getting a Second Chance at Life

This pain in my heart, it drives me mad.
Sometimes I feel so good, again, I feel so bad.

—Willie Dixon,
"This Pain in My Heart"

My treatment for depression has been a journey. As I'm sure is true for most people who battle the disease, the path seldom has been straight. There have been twists and turns, ups and downs. The roller-coaster ride can be frustrating and discouraging for anyone, but especially for those of us who, like many black men, find it difficult to accept that clinical depression is their problem and that medication and psychotherapy are the solutions.

Many people experience a serious bout of depression brought on by a triggering event such as divorce or a death in the family. The majority will ride out the sadness, relying on the old saw that time heals all wounds. A relative few will get into therapy and take medication. They start feeling like their former selves. They end the therapy, stop taking the medication, and never fall into another depression. They are cured. For many others, however, depression is a chronic illness. It needs no triggering event. It can descend on you when you feel happy, like a whirlwind out of a clear blue sky. Therapy and medication may force it into retreat, but depression lurks in the brain until given a chance to return. I'm in the chronic group.

I didn't go into treatment for depression eight years ago expecting miracles. In fact, I didn't think any miracles were needed. It's just as well that those were my attitudes, because they spared me disappointment. Nothing I consider miraculous happened to me. I do believe that what happened saved my life. What happened in the course of my treatment also brought about some fundamental changes in the way I live.

In fact, I don't believe it is an overstatement to say that finally getting help for my depression gave me a second chance at life.

As I said in the previous chapter, medication almost immediately began making a difference in the way I felt. Perhaps the placebo effect allowed me to feel the benefits before the medicines were even metabolized by my body. Given time, the medications did their jobs. They were the parachutes that broke my emotional and physical free fall.

Anti-anxiety medications came first and were essential in getting me from the crisis stage to the point at which I was stabilized. They were like Advil that soothed my inflamed emotions, lowered my emotional temperature, and allowed healing to begin.

These medications would be short-term measures for some people. That wasn't the case for me. I've never gone completely off anti-anxiety medication since I began taking Klonopin. That's mainly because it is part of a two- or three-pill cocktail I need to ensure a good night's sleep. I didn't like the idea of having to take these medicines every night. It smacked of dependency, if not outright addiction. There were many times when I stayed up late into the night, waiting until I felt I could not keep my eyes open any longer. Then I would get into bed. This strategy failed, however. I might fall asleep quickly, but I woke a short time later and I could not get back to sleep.

Dr. Serravezza sympathized with my concern about needing the pills. But she said she was more concerned about my need to get a sound night's sleep and wake up rested in the morning. There were various strategies that I might try to improve my sleep, but if medication was the only thing that worked, then I should take the medication.

I've come to accept that, and I've been willing to try new medications when necessary. At first, Klonopin was the medication I took primarily for anxiety and as needed to help me sleep. Eventually, Neurontin was added to the mix. Dr. Serravezza explained that this drug was not developed as a treatment for depression, but there had been some success in using it to treat depression by decreasing anxiety. In 2002, news reports appeared on allegations linking Neurontin to suicides by young people who took it as an antidepressant. I did some research and found that debate over whether Neurontin actually caused suicide was in its early stages; the question remained very much open. In addition, the cases that were the basis for the charge involved young people for whom Neurontin was the primary or only antidepressant prescribed. In my case, it was only used as another sleep aid. I discussed the issue briefly with Dr. Serravezza. She agreed with the conclusion I had reached based on my own investigation.

My medication regimen was effective for about four years. But then something changed. I had difficulty sleeping even while taking the medication. The short periods of sleep I got were fitful. I was tormented by bizarre dreams that ran through my head over and over again, like video loops. In one recurring dream, I was doing carpentry work. I would saw and plane wood, and as I did this I realized that the wood actually felt pain with each cut or scrape. I couldn't understand how I knew this. The wood didn't cry out or writhe like a live thing. Yet I knew in my heart that I was hurting the wood. This scene and the sense of guilt it instilled in me would repeat themselves throughout the night. This was no recipe for restful sleep.

Dr. Serravezza suggested that I try Seroquel. She said it was used as an antipsychotic, but in the small dose she would prescribe for me its value would be to help me sleep soundly. It has allowed me to fall into a sleep uninterrupted by dreams. Before the depression and the anxiety, slumber for me was like a second, better life. Most nights were full of dreams of sweetness and adventure. Now there are pleasurable dreams once in a while, but most nights are like resting in a darkened movie theater where the screen is forever blank. I'm grateful for what dreams may come, but I'll settle for restful nights.

The anti-anxiety medications I took were not just about getting sleep. Clinical depression is often accompanied by an anxiety disorder. That's not surprising. If we lose hope and fall into pessimism, that feeds a constant state of worry and fear. Anxiety becomes the fever that never breaks. It is a low-grade fever most of the time, but sometimes it spikes.

I knew the anxiety fever long before I knew anything about depression. Most people who've known me over the years probably would say I'm a patient, deliberate person. That might have been my outward appearance, but something quite different was going on inside. Often I felt pressured and in turmoil, as if there was never enough time to do all the things I needed to get done.

Some people saw through the façade. One of them was Ben Hamilton. Ben came to my rescue when I was restoring my grandparents' farmhouse, the project that became the subject of my first book. He knows just about everything there is to know about houses. Ben also is one of the wisest and most observant men I've ever known.

He spotted my frustration when I couldn't get the knack of small things I was trying to do, like cutting a straight line with a circular saw. "You always seem to be rushing," Ben told me. "You're even in a hurry to take your time." He suggested that I step back from what I was doing, take a deep breath, and calm down; there are times when you can get things done faster by slowing down.

That's good advice, but it's not always easy to follow. I think it's especially difficult for an African American man who's feeling the pressure of being society's perpetual suspect. I've felt that pressure, and I'm sure many other black men also feel it. It's the feeling that everything about you is subject to suspicion because of what you are. You internalize the way you believe the world sees you, making that negative image a part of yourself. It causes you to raise the same questions about yourself—whether you're qualified; whether you're capable of doing the job—no matter how much you succeed. We're especially vulnerable to this kind of thinking if our minds are clouded by depression.

After I bounced back from the 1996 breakdown at work and reached the point of stability, I no longer took anti-anxiety medication regularly. Instead, Dr. Serravezza had me take it as I needed it. I've tried various relaxation techniques over the years. Most are very rudimentary forms of yoga or meditation—stretching and mental imaging exercises designed to relieve stress. The idea that I suffered from an anxiety disorder hadn't even entered my mind when I first tried these techniques. Rather, I used them because I thought they might help me perform under pressure on the tennis court. Eventually I applied them to the stress I experienced in everyday life. They helped sometimes. But I know now that I needed medication to help me calm down and take that deep breath Ben advised me to take. It allowed me time to think. Without that, the new way of thinking I gained through treatment would have been useless.

■ ■ ■

Dealing with anxiety was important, of course. But the main event on my fight card was my bout with clinical depression. I've talked some about the importance of antidepressants. They have been an essential part of my treatment. But the "talk therapy" with Dr. Serravezza has been just as important. Studies show that this is true for depression in general. The 1999 Surgeon General's Report on Mental Health says treatment of depression with medication is effective, and talk therapy also is effective. The best results, however, have come from a combination of the two.

Talk therapy is especially important for those who aren't apt to talk about their emotional problems. Men in general, and black men in particular, fall into that category. When I interviewed Dr. Sandra Walker, the psychoanalyst from Seattle, she talked about psychoanalysis as a way of dealing with emotional wounds involving race, because so much of what we feel about race remains unspoken and buried inside us. Of course, to get African American men to talk about race—or talk about any sensitive subject, for that matter—

therapists must convince us that talking will help and that the therapists provide a safe place to talk.

"Racism and heritage from slavery in this country have ongoing meanings for African Americans *and* for whites," Dr. Walker told me. "Everybody, individually, has an individual experience and a psychological representation of the past. Many of the African American patients I work with have experienced narcissistic injury—injury to their sense of self—as a result of racism. How that affects individuals really depends on a lot of things, in terms of their biopsychosocial experience and makeup. But it's a factor. For African Americans who are seeking treatment and help, providing a setting where those issues can come up comfortably is an important part of being able to be helpful."

As I've said before, the best way to change the way people think about something is to change the way they talk about it. By the same token, you can't change the way you think, if you refuse to *talk* about the way you think.

Dr. Serravezza helped me talk about the way I thought and about the way depression influenced my thinking. Without this piece of the treatment puzzle, I believe, using medication to ease the influence of depression would have created a vacuum. I had to have the possibility of a different way of thinking about myself to fill that void.

Depression makes you think negatively, and I certainly did a lot of that. I eventually understood how that kind of thinking dominated my life. I worried about becoming the person I *didn't* want to be, instead of putting my energy into becoming the person I *wanted* to be. I tried not to be the caricature of the black male who is so widely feared and detested in our society. Specifically, I was desperate not to be the kind of father my father was. I didn't want to not support my sons. I didn't want to not encourage them. I didn't want to not protect them. I didn't want to not be there at all for them.

Beginning my recovery from depression was the first step toward understanding that all this "not" was not the way I had to live. I knew I wasn't giving my sons what I wanted to give them and what they needed from me. It wasn't enough that I was not the kind of father my father was. My depression so focused me on the possibility of making mistakes that my relationship with my sons was more about not inflicting my failings on them than it was about giving them any positives I had to offer.

I was creating a hole in my sons' lives. Most often, the evidence of this was unspoken; it was on their faces. I could see the disappointment when I didn't have the energy or enough interest to do things with them that I didn't feel obligated to do, to do things with them just for the enjoyment of doing it with them. I could see the looks of fear when I boiled with pure resentment over having to meet my responsibilities to them. I had promised myself that I would never hit my children; they would never get the whippings I got when I was a child. I've lived up to the spirit of the promise if not the letter. There may have been two or three occasions when I've struck one of them on the bottom, once, with my open hand, to get them to stop doing something after words failed to do the job. The times I've grabbed one of them forcefully by the arm number a half dozen or less. But there have been many times when, in one of my moods, I've used words that could cut them more deeply and wound them more permanently than any belt could. When I look back on that now, I see that refusing to use corporal punishment was about withholding what I considered to be negative behavior from them. It wasn't about disciplining them in a way that let them see that I loved them. I can see that now, but I couldn't see it then.

I began to see these things when I started dealing with my depression. My eyes were really opened, though, during a parent-teacher conference with my thirteen-year-old son. The meeting was going as expected. My son was doing well with his schoolwork. He got along well with his classmates. His behavior was good for the most part, the only problem being a tendency to be easily distracted when he should have been concentrating on classwork.

The teacher asked if I had any questions. I asked a couple. Then the teacher said my son had something to say. He stood up and began talking in a voice choked with emotion.

"Dad," he said. "I don't feel safe. You don't hug me. You don't tell me you love me. I need those things to feel safe. Most of the time you just seem to be mad at me, and I worry that it's something I'm doing to make you not want to be around me. I love you a lot and I really need to know that you love me."

He was crying. My eyes were wet, too. The teacher asked my son if he needed a hug right then. "Yes," he said.

We stood together and embraced. I pulled my son tight against me. "I do love you," I said. "I want you to know that I love you."

I felt hot with many shames. I was ashamed that I had not made it clear to my son how much I loved him. I was ashamed that he felt he could not tell me how that made him feel. I was ashamed that he was able to tell a teacher who had known him only for a few months what he couldn't bring himself to tell me. I felt ashamed for those reasons and more.

But what shamed me most was that I understood why my son couldn't confide in me. He had seen me shut down emotionally too often. And the only emotion he had seen break through the wall I built around myself was anger. Why risk trying to get me to open up? Why chip away at the dam when the dam was the only thing holding back a river of resentment?

Fortunately, by the time my son felt compelled to ask me to open up, I was ready. I was ready because my depression was receding by then, thanks to medication and therapy. I no longer felt hopeless. I didn't believe that I was doomed and my sons were doomed and there was nothing I could do for myself or for them. I no longer believed that the best I could do for them was not to be my father. I believed that showing my sons I loved them was important and would make a difference in their lives.

No doubt, most people would say these things are part of Parenting 101. They are things you have to know and believe before you even consider bringing a child into the world. I agree. These are precepts parents must cling to. But, depression can loosen our grip on those things we hold most precious, even our ideals and our desires. Once the depression begins to ease, the things we let slip away are not regained all at once. They come back to us gradually.

And sometimes it takes a push to make us reach out for a lost piece of ourselves. Hearing my son's tearful words in that parent-teacher conference was one of the pushes I needed.

Understanding my own depression made me more optimistic about my sons. It also has made me worry about them in a new way. I worry that the illness will be handed down from me to them. I watch for signs of it, looking for the child I was at their age, and looking for younger versions of the adult I became. Is it a bad sign that one of them likes to nap during the day? What about the one who doesn't sleep much at night? Is the one who shows enthusiasm for almost nothing depressed? Is the one who's enthusiastic about almost everything manic? Mostly, I know, they are just being kids.

But I watch them. If I see them struggling with their emotions, I talk to them. I let them know they can talk to me about such problems. I talk to them about mine. I tell them that there are times when I feel really sad, and that I talk to a doctor and take pills and that those things help me feel better.

And, most of all, I tell them that I love them.

◼ ◼ ◼

Black men have a reputation regarding our relationships with women. The reputation goes something like this: When it comes to caring about women, black men can talk the talk, but we don't always walk the walk. We will tell anyone within earshot how much we love women, how we adore them. Some of us will even throw in a word or two about how much we respect women. But the way we actually treat them is a different matter. It starts with the first women in our lives: our mothers. We carry on about how much our mothers mean to us. We say we care more about our mothers than we care about ourselves. If we're playing the dozens—the competition of escalating personal insults—the way to up the ante from conventional warfare to an exchange of nuclear weapons is to start talking about each other's mamas. Yet our mothers are the first women we disappoint. We disappoint them when we don't grow up to be the men they raised us to be, and we especially disappoint them when we don't treat women the way they wish they had been treated.

The way we treat women has little to do with love and nothing to do with respect. We shower them with what looks like love to get from them what we want, which is sex first and anything else they're willing to give thereafter. After that, we move on. We refuse to be tied down, even by children. We see relationships in the short term—only long enough to have our needs and desires met. The future? What's that? We don't plan on having one for ourselves, much less for anyone connected to us.

This is a portrait of black men painted with the broadest of broad brushes. Certainly it does not capture all black men; I dare say it doesn't apply to most, though I've met plenty of women who would say their own unscientific survey shows otherwise. It is a stereotype. But it's a stereotype that is more likely to become reality when clinical depression is involved.

Let's not go a word further without saying this in no uncertain terms: Clinical depression is not always an explanation and is never an excuse for an African American man—or any man, for that matter—to mistreat a woman. It can be a factor, however. If it is a factor, the problem can't be solved without addressing the depression.

I know from experience that depression affects relationships. In fact, the closer and more important the relationship is, the more damage depression will do. It happened with my sons, and it has happened with the women in my life. It's clear to me now that depression was a driving force in the three stages I would go through in my relationships with women.

Romance blooms in the first stage. It involves the initial infatuation and the thrill of pursuit. For any man, sexual conquest may mark the high point of this phase of a relationship. That's particularly true for a man in the throes of depression. Sex answers a need for some sense of self-esteem and validation of masculinity—no matter how shallow; and it is a source of pleasure, a sanctuary from suffering. Obsessive behavior, which often accompanies depression, can be mistaken for an intense romantic attentiveness. And depression so magnifies the importance of this relatively trivial and transitory phase of a relationship that it destines whatever follows to be a disappointment.

Love begins to bear fruit in the second stage, if things get that far. This is where those things that make a relationship last take hold—mutual values and interests, communications, trust, respect, love. The odds are against couples reaching this stage, must less flourishing in it. This can be tough territory for any relationship. When mine reached this point, depression was the determined saboteur lurking in the shadows. It worked against everything that was needed to make the relationship work. I had neither interest nor energy to invest. I was emotionally absent, except for that eternally simmering resentment. Worst of all, no matter how desperate I might be for a relationship to work, I saw no reason to hope that it would. I did not believe that making it work would make me any happier. Nothing would. I was destined to be unhappy.

Breakup is the final phase. For me, it didn't matter that I believed this ending was inevitable: It was always devastating. By this point, depression was both master chef and the only diner at the feast. It created and consumed everything the relationship was about. It became the emotional version of the elusive perpetual-motion machine. Nothing contributed to the end of a relationship like my depression. Nothing drove me deeper into depression than the end of a relationship.

It may be possible for a relationship to flourish with one of the people involved suffering through the depths of depression, but I can't imagine it. The depression has to be dealt with if the relationship is to have any chance at all. Looking back now, I can only guess that my desperation to find some way out of depression, perhaps the belief that the right woman would just pull me out despite myself, was the only thing that allowed me to open up enough to even begin a relationship. That was a false hope, of course, but it was the only kind of hope I could muster.

Getting treatment for my depression created hope. It gave my marriage a chance to work, even as it was all but ended. Something strange happened after Claire and I decided to go our separate ways: We started to get along better. We became friends, who helped each other whenever help was needed. We could disagree without being disagreeable. We were living apart, but somehow we had gotten closer than we had been in years.

The element of our relationship that improved the most was the thing that both of us always considered the most important, no matter what we thought about each other. Our partnership as parents was stronger than ever. I have to say that the biggest difference was my willingness to take full part at last. Not only had the way I treated my sons changed, the way I treated Claire was different too. I was more open to her, more willing to listen to her concerns and, even, to talk about mine.

Someone once said that for every complex problem there is a simple solution that doesn't work. Some might say that the simple answer to why Claire and I suddenly started getting along was that it was much easier to get along at a distance. Others might say our relationship improved because the pressure was off. We were no longer dealing with the destructive dynamics of a failing marriage. There could be numerous explanations that follow in the same vein. My own explanation is similarly simple, but I believe it is the correct one. Things began to change for the better between us because I got help for my depression.

When we sat down and began talking about whether we should give the marriage another chance, Claire asked me why I thought we should try. "We've been getting along so well lately," I said. "I think things are different now that the depression is under control. I believe I'm different."

"Different how?" she asked.

"I'm more open, for one thing," I said. "I think we're communicating much better. I'm willing to make a commitment to make the marriage work. And I believe now that making the marriage work will make a difference in our lives. The depression stood in the way of that."

"The depression is only one component of this," Claire said. "It's important, but it's not the only reason the marriage didn't work before. There are other things that have to change."

I said, "I know that. But it seems to me that enough has changed already for us to make a new start. But the bottom line for me is the difference we can make for the boys. It would be a shame to continue putting them through this if there's a chance we don't have to."

"I've always said that," she said.

We both knew that what we were talking about was giving a great gift to our children. It may be the greatest gift we can give them.

I believe it is a gift that many men wish for but find themselves unable to give. Depression deprives them of the ability to give it. And I believe this is especially true for black men. From where we stand, it requires a great deal of faith and optimism to believe that things will turn out well for us and the people we love. We must overcome the evidence that says our fate is out of our hands, that we can do our best, yet wind up relegated to a place among society's worst. Add clinical depression to this, and what chance is there? At various points in my life, the answer was plain to me: No chance. No chance at all.

␣␣␣

Having laid out the story of my battle with depression—a story not so much of success, but of survival—I can imagine what many people will say about it. It's obvious he has learned his lesson, they will say. He can see the dividing line between his life with untreated clinical depression and his life with treatment. And he knows on which side of that line he must stay.

It's not that easy.

A 2003 policy brief funded by the W. K. Kellogg Foundation says studies show that the stigma of depression and other factors push African American men to drop out of treatment for depression. This only makes the illness more dangerous for us. I learned that when, after deciding in 1997 to end my sessions with Dr. Serravezza and to stop taking medication, I soon became as depressed as ever and was again seriously contemplating suicide.

Why, one might ask, would someone who knows he has a life-threatening illness stop seeing the doctor and taking the medication that keeps him alive? I did for a number of reasons. The first was that after being in treatment for about a year I really felt better. I felt I had treated the illness long enough. I felt I was cured. I was wrong.

Another reason is that some aspects of treatment aren't a whole lot of fun. On a very basic level, it takes discipline to follow a routine every day, even one as simple as taking certain pills in a certain number and at a certain time. Side effects are another issue. Earlier, I mentioned the strategy of taking "medication vacations" once in a while, to have a few days without the side effects that interfered with things I enjoyed doing. That was not enough—I wanted to be rid of even the most minor side effect.

I can't think of many reasons that would make the risk of going off medication for clinical depression worthwhile. It has to be a pretty stark choice. Derrick Adkins, the 400-meter hurdler who won a gold medal in the 1996 Summer Olympics in Atlanta, faced such a choice. He suffered from depression for years. He wasn't diagnosed and placed on medication until the spring before his gold-medal summer. The medication got his depression under control. The problem, however, was that it interfered with his athletic performance. World-class athletes constantly look for an edge on the competition. Most find it through training or nutrition. A few resort to illegal performance-enhancing drugs. Derrick Adkins was taking a drug that was essential to his emotional health, but it hampered his athletic abilities. He made the decision to go off his medication long enough to train for and compete in the Olympics. Preparing for the Olympics had become the focus of his life. In an interview with the *Atlanta Journal-Constitution* reporter Mike Fish in the summer of 2000, Adkins said that going off his medication was "a scary thing to do, but I was so obsessed with the Olympics."

Like most people, I didn't need a chance to perform on the world stage to be tempted to go off my medication. For one thing, I wanted to enjoy playing tennis the way I used to. I wasn't any great player, but I entered local and state tournaments, won a few titles over the years, and even spent vacations traveling to play in national tournaments just for the sheer enjoyment of it. Like Derrick Adkins, I found that one of my medications cut into my athletic performance. It affected motor skills, especially hand-eye coordination. Unlike Adkins, though, I didn't have that much performance to cut into. During the first year of my treatment, before Dr. Serravezza and I fine-tuned my medication regimen, I sometimes had trouble playing at all.

So I rationalized. I told myself that the medication kept me from enjoying my life as much as I wanted to. (Of course, the medication was one of the reasons I even felt there was a possibility of enjoying life.) And I told myself that I was feeling so much better that I didn't need the medication.

It didn't take long for me to see that I was mistaken. I began to sink into depression again. My anxiety began to spike again. This time, at least, I understood what was happening. I no longer considered thoughts of suicide as nothing more than morbid fantasy. I knew they were real signs of danger.

I resumed taking my medications and seeing Dr. Serravezza on a regular schedule, though our sessions' frequency decreased as time passed. I felt better with the passage of time. As I said earlier, I didn't become immune to sadness, but I was much better equipped to cope with feeling sad.

My emotional coping skills in general have been sharpened. There is the matter of Christmas, for instance. I don't think I've really had the Christmas spirit since childhood—maybe since not too long after I found out that there is no Santa Claus. For years, it was the most depressing time of the year for me. Partly this was because of the onset of winter. But worse were the stress, anxiety, and disappointment of what Christmas had become for me. And I was pushed further down by the apparent good cheer of everyone around me.

What was wrong with me that I was immune to the infectious holiday happiness?

Well, I'm not exactly Scrooge after the visit of the Christmas ghosts, but my attitude has changed. I take my joy in Christmas where I find it, as in the delight and excitement my sons feel when they pull something from under the tree, tear off the wrapping paper, and find that gift they've been dropping hints about since September. I certainly don't allow anyone else's happiness to be the source of my unhappiness, at Christmastime or any other time.

Much of what I've written here about my difficulty in coming to terms with my depression has concerned my ignorance of the disease for much of my life. As I've said, I wasn't brought up in a culture where mental illness was discussed. I may have given the impression that I crossed some imaginary line from ignorance to knowledge and then I was on my way. That's not what happened. The truth is that I needed more than knowledge to really start changing and start healing. The genesis of the change came one Sunday evening, when I heard the soft Southern drawl of the former first lady Rosalynn Carter floating from my radio.

That was in the early spring of 1998. I was finishing some work on the restoration of my grandparents' farmhouse in Jackson. It was time to head back to Atlanta. I was putting away tools and packing up for the drive. The radio was tuned to the local Georgia Public Radio station, and a weekly show called *The Infinite Mind* was on. The show was about mental health. I listened regularly. It wasn't just because I had been diagnosed with depression. The workings of the mind had always interested me. This show presented discussions of the subject that were informative and accessible.

Rosalynn Carter was the guest that Sunday evening. She talked about her public work on behalf of people with mental illness. It had started in the early 1970s when her husband, Jimmy, was governor and she was Georgia's first lady. Her efforts increased when Jimmy Carter became president. And they did not abate after he left office. If anything, she became more active once she returned to private life and helped her husband establish the Carter Center in Atlanta. As the leader of the Carter Center's Mental Health Program she devoted herself to fighting for better mental health care wherever she could find a way to fight, whether in African huts or the halls of Congress.

Mrs. Carter spent a good part of the interview talking about growing up in a small Georgia town and seeing people suffering from mental illness. Most people in the community did what they could to protect these people, she said, but there was little concept of treatment that might actually help them live fuller lives. I could relate to Mrs. Carter's experiences.

Then she mentioned one of her pet projects: the Rosalynn Carter Mental Health Journalism Fellowship Program. It allowed journalists to spend a year working on projects to enlighten the public about mental health in some way. At the same time, the journalists would learn things about mental health that would be with them for the rest of their careers and, perhaps, have a positive impact on the way the journalists around them reported on mental health. Mrs. Carter said anyone interested should contact the Carter Center.

This was not one of those cushy sabbaticals that journalists and other professionals dream about falling into—one of those take-a-year-off-and-think-great-thoughts programs in which all you have to accomplish is to feel that you're a better person at the end of the year. This was a don't-quit-your-day-job fellowship that expected its fellows to produce something tangible. It appealed to me.

It was already late in the selection process for the coming year when I heard Mrs. Carter's interview. I submitted an application right at the deadline. Eventually I got a nice response saying I hadn't made the cut this time, but encouraging me to try again for the following year. I did, and, lo and behold, I was one of the six fellows chosen for the 1999–2000 program. My proposal was to write a book about access to mental health care in the African American community.

The focus of the project narrowed as the year progressed. My initial proposal was too big a bite for me to swallow, even over the course of a year or more. The fellowship also motivated me to change my focus at the newspaper. I moved from the editorial board to the features department, where mental health became my beat. The Carter Center fellowship generated contacts and story ideas that I used to write articles for the newspaper. Meanwhile I gathered material for the book.

Finally, my topic evolved into something manageable. It would be about black men and depression. That was a natural for me, but I didn't tell anyone that. Whenever anyone asked me why I had chosen that subject, I said it was something that interested me and that I had not seen anyone else take up. This was the truth, but it left out the most important truth, of course. I was still afraid to tell people that I knew the subject I planned to write about from personal experience.

This must sound amazing to most people. I was in an environment where I was learning to fight the stigma attached to mental illness, while surrounded by people who cared about the issue. If there was any place to feel comfortable talking about my fight with depression, this should have been it. Yet I couldn't break through my own fear of being identified as someone with a mental illness. I couldn't bring myself to talk about it.

This reticence was not without cause, of course. For example, I was talking about my Carter Center fellowship with some coworkers at the newspaper one day. Someone asked me what the book I was working on was about. I gave the evasive half truth that had become my standard answer to that question.

"It's about access to mental health care in the African American community," I said. "Especially for black men."

"I hope you're not writing from personal experience!" someone else piped up.

I kept silent as everyone around me laughed.

"Of course it's from personal experience," another colleague said. "Everyone knows John is nuts!"

More laughter.

There is prejudice against people with mental illness, even among those who should know better. Mostly it's an unthinking kind of prejudice. It's not that people hate those who suffer. They are uncomfortable with the subject, to say nothing of the people. They don't see it as a "real" illness. They make jokes and laugh about it on reflex. If I had said I was writing a book about access to cancer treatment in the African American community, especially among black men, there would have been no snide remarks and no laughter. The way I saw people stigmatize mental illness reinforced my embarrassment. So I kept silent about myself.

Then, while giving a progress report on my project before other fellows and advisers to the Carter Center's mental health program, I broke through my fear. I was talking about the articles I had written about mental illness for the newspaper. I said the most effective pieces were those in which people with mental illnesses told their own stories. Unfortunately, I added, there weren't that many people who were willing to talk about what it's like to suffer from a mental illness. "I was going to say that I don't want to be critical of the people who won't go public, but I think they could do a lot of good if they would talk," I said. "But then I thought, 'Look who's talking,' because I haven't been willing to talk about my own experiences. So I am going to talk. The book I'm writing isn't just about black men and depression. It's also about my own experiences as someone who suffered from depression before finally getting help."

So there it was, the first time I had volunteered that information to anyone outside my family. I eventually went public, writing about my depression in my newspaper. The truth was out there, at long last.

Yes, I consider myself a survivor of depression, someone who during his illness contemplated suicide many times and came frighteningly close to completing the act. I look back now and rejoice that I didn't take my life. I rejoice that I didn't take undeserved "revenge" on people who love and care about me. In the warped way of thinking brought on by depression, suicide is an act of vengeance against the world we've come to hate, a world we can't stand to live in. There's no reason to inflict that kind of damage on the hearts of those around us. I'm glad I didn't.

And I'm glad I didn't go through with suicide because, if I had, I would have missed the joy I experience with my sons—the joy of a job well done after working side by side on the farm with my eldest, Joakim; the joy of playing tennis with my middle son, Gabriel; the joy of dining out with my youngest son, Steven, at his favorite fast-food restaurant. These are just a few of the joys that depression lessened for me and suicide would have denied me forever.

I've come a long way in eight years. I wouldn't say that I'm transformed. I'm not a better person. I'm merely less sick than I once was, and I'm therefore fitter to strive to be the kind of person I'd like to be. I still have my worries and my sadness, but I have hope. I'm open to joy. When depression strikes, it no longer catches me unawares. I know that I can fight it and that the fight is not mine alone. There is help. I know where to find it. I know how to ask for it.

I am not alone.

I am not afraid.

I am not ashamed.

NINE

Breaking the Chains
of Depression

I'm going down to the river take along my rocking chair.
And if the blues don't leave me. I'll rock on away from there.

—Richard M. Jones,

"Trouble in Mind"

Untreated clinical depression is modern-day slavery. It robs people of their freedom and limits their choices as effectively as the "peculiar institution" ever did. For those who find themselves in the bondage of depression, the reports on mental health issued by the U.S. Surgeon General constitute an Emancipation Proclamation. Like Abraham Lincoln's edict, the reports on mental health do not and cannot provide immediate freedom for anyone. But also like Lincoln's proclamation, the reports declare the nation's duty—even its moral obligation—to free those who are enslaved by mental illness.

As I said at the beginning of this book, Dr. David Satcher broke new ground when he issued the 1999 Surgeon General's Report on Mental Health. He used his position to inform the nation of the scope of the mental health challenges we face and of our ability to meet those challenges if we develop the will to use the increasingly effective tools science is providing us. And he emphasized the importance of making those resources available across all the nation's dividing lines.

David Satcher is an African American physician who has devoted his professional life to improving public health for all Americans, but he has been particularly passionate about working on behalf of minority communities for which our nation has failed to provide adequate access to health care.

When I spoke with Dr. Satcher after a speech he gave in Atlanta about mental health, I told him it seemed that taking on the issue was a personal mission for him. I asked why.

One of the things he has sought to do throughout his career in medicine, including the time he spent as Surgeon General, he said, was to eliminate the disparity between the health care available to people in minority communities and the care available to others. "There's disparity across the health care system," he told me, "but there is no wider disparity than there is regarding mental health care."

I asked him the same question in the summer of 2003, after he had completed his term as Surgeon General and taken the helm of the new National Center for Primary Care at Morehouse School of Medicine. This time, however, I wanted to know whether personal experiences shaped his attitude toward mental illness. Yes, he said, mentioning an alcoholic grandfather, and an aunt who was found dead under circumstances that the family seemed determined to keep "very murky."

"I was young and didn't understand," Dr. Satcher said. "But even though I didn't understand, I felt the aura that surrounded the issue of mental illness; it was something people wouldn't talk about. Neither of my parents finished grade school, so it probably wasn't something they could even try to explain to me."

Before his term expired at the end of February 2002, Dr. Satcher issued several supplements to his original report on mental health. "Mental Health: Culture, Race, Ethnicity," the supplemental report released in August 2001, includes important information on the impact of mental illnesses, including depression, on African Americans. In the months leading up to the report's release, Dr. Satcher often spoke about a mental health crisis in black communities. He saw the dramatic increase in suicides among young black men as the prime marker of the burgeoning problem.

The supplement on culture, race, and ethnicity emphasizes that much of what went into the body of the report also applies to minority populations. For example, there's this piece of advice: "The efficacy of mental health treatment is so well documented that the Surgeon General made this single, explicit recommendation for all people: *Seek help if you have a mental health problem or think you have symptoms of a mental disorder.*

"The recommendation to seek help is particularly vital, considering *the majority of people with diagnosable disorders, regardless of race or ethnicity, do not receive treatment.*"

According to the report, the best available research indicates that—after adjusting for socioeconomic status—the rate of mental illnesses such as depression for African Americans is similar to that for whites. That means, for example, that the rate of mental illness for poor blacks is compared with the rate for poor whites, since poverty is a recognized risk factor for mental health problems. As noted previously, there are experts who argue with this conclusion. The Surgeon General's Report concedes that there is little mental health research that looks specifically at African Americans. It notes that African Americans are overrepresented among the homeless, the incarcerated, and the institutionalized, and that while these groups are known to have higher rates of mental illness they are not included in surveys intended to establish baselines for the rates of mental illness for various populations. (It should be noted, by the way, that not only are African Americans overrepresented in these groups, but men are overrepresented among those African Americans.) Despite these and other factors that bring into question the statistics being used, the few studies that have been done provide no indication that there are significant racial or ethnic differences in the rates of mental illness.

While the report is carefully equivocal concerning whether African Americans have higher rates of depression and other mental illnesses than the rest of the U.S. population, it is emphatic about the disproportionate impact mental illnesses have on blacks and other minorities.

The supplemental report

finds that racial and ethnic minorities collectively experience a greater disability burden from mental illness than do whites. This higher level of burden stems from minorities receiving less care and poorer quality of care, rather than from their illnesses being inherently more severe or prevalent in the community.

... Because of disparities in mental health services, a disproportionate number of minorities with mental illnesses do not fully benefit from, or contribute to, the opportunities and prosperity of our society. This preventable disability from mental illnesses exacts a high societal toll and affects all Americans. Most troubling of all, the burden for minorities is growing. They are becoming more populous, all the while experiencing continuing inequality of income and economic opportunity. Racial and ethnic minorities in the United States face a social and economic environment of inequality that includes greater exposure to racism and discrimination, violence, and poverty, all of which take a toll on mental health.

"Reducing or eliminating these disparities requires a steadfast commitment by all sectors of American society," the report maintains, going on to make recommendations on how to accomplish this.

- **Continue to expand the science base.** "The science base regarding racial and ethnic minority mental health is limited but growing. . . . Several large epidemiological studies that include significant samples of racial and ethnic minorities have recently been initiated or completed. These surveys, when combined with smaller, ethnic-specific epidemiological surveys, may help resolve some of the uncertainties about the extent of mental illness among racial and ethnic groups."
- **Improve access to treatment.** "Simply put, the Nation's health systems must work to bring mental health services to where the people are. Many racial and ethnic minorities live in areas where general health care and specialty mental health care are in short

supply. One major course of action is to *improve geographic availability of mental health services.* Innovative strategies for training providers, delivering services, creating incentives for providers to work in underserved areas, and strengthening the public health safety net promise to provide greater geographic access to mental health services for those in need."

Lower barriers to mental health care. "The foremost barriers that deter racial and ethnic minorities from reaching treatment are the cost of services, the fragmented organization of these services, and societal stigma toward mental illness. . . . [The report] aims to make services more accessible and appropriate to racial and ethnic minorities, . . . encourages mental health coverage for millions of Americans who are uninsured, and . . . maintains that parity, or equivalence, between mental health coverage and other health coverage is an affordable and effective strategy for reducing racial and ethnic disparities."

Improve the quality of mental health services. "Above all, improving the quality of mental health care is a vital goal for the nation. Persons with mental illness who receive quality care are more likely to stay in treatment and to have better outcomes. . . . To be most effective, *treatments always need to be individualized in the clinical setting according to each patient's age, gender, race, ethnicity, and culture.* . . . At the same time, research is needed on several fronts, such as how to adapt evidence-based treatments to maximize their appeal and effectiveness for racial and ethnic minorities."

Support capacity development. "This Supplement encourages all mental health professionals to develop their skills in tailoring treatment to age, gender, race, ethnicity, and culture. In addition, because minorities are dramatically underrepresented among mental health providers, researchers, administrators, policy makers, and consumer and family organizations, racial and ethnic minorities are encouraged to enter the mental health field. Training programs and funding sources also need to work toward equitable racial and ethnic minority representation in all these groups."

▪ **Promote mental health.** "Mental health promotion and mental illness prevention can improve the health of a community and the Nation. Because mental health is adversely affected by chronic social conditions such as poverty, community violence, racism, and discrimination, the reduction of these adverse conditions is quite likely to be vital to improving the mental health of racial and ethnic minorities."

David Satcher wants one of his legacies as Surgeon General to be improved mental health among African Americans and improved access to mental health care for African Americans who need help. With his reports on mental health, he has shown America how to do it. Now the nation must show that it has the necessary will to carry it out.

▪ ▪ ▪

I look back on my experience with depression and realize how fortunate I've been. I am surviving a life-threatening illness. I received top-quality therapy and the most effective medications on the market, with most of the costs covered by health insurance available through my job. I didn't suffer the stigmatization I feared. Family, friends, and most coworkers were supportive, not judgmental. Such an outcome should be available to all Americans who suffer from mental illness. It is not. That must change.

My ideas—which grow out of my own struggles with depression—on how to bring about the needed changes pretty much parallel Dr. Satcher's. But I would add one major component to the Surgeon General's recommendations.

That major component is a single-payer national health care system. We'll never reach the goal of providing adequate health care for all Americans without taking this step. This is especially true of coverage for mental health care. Right now, only about 6 percent of all health care spending in the United States goes for mental health treatment. That is short shrift. We must begin to balance the scales so that our health care spending reflects our health care needs.

Overall, the private health insurance industry has a prejudice against paying for treatment of mental illness. Studies show that providing mental health coverage will not significantly raise the cost for insurers. Yet many in the industry cling to the idea that mental health-care costs are a bottomless pit, which will bankrupt health insurance companies. They maintain that mental illness is too easy to fake or too hard to cure.

In my experience, there's no attraction in faking an illness in order to get money to buy medications that will help only if you're really sick and that can cause unpleasant side effects. As for whether people with mental illness ever are "cured," yes, some are. They undergo treatment or take medication for a time and don't need it again. However, many others must continue treatment or medication for a very long time, possibly for the rest of their lives. But this is true of people with asthma, heart disease, diabetes, or any of the many other chronic illnesses for whose treatment insurance companies routinely pay.

By eliminating the profit motive, a national health care system would eliminate the private insurers' lame excuses, especially the excuse that mental illness is too costly because treatment is so long term. With such a system, the costs and benefits of paying for the best possible treatment for mental illness would be apparent. First, good treatment would allow afflicted people to lead self-sufficient, productive lives, contributing to the economy with their labor and to government coffers with their tax dollars. And, of course, paying for properly diagnosed mental health problems up front is far less expensive than allowing illnesses to go untreated until they become florid and require more drastic and costly steps, such as institutionalization. A single-payer system also would make the stigma attached to mental illness less of a barrier to treatment. Fewer people would be involved in approving and paying for treatment. Employers, in particular, would be taken out of the loop, which would ease people's fear that treatment for mental illness will cost them their jobs or invite discrimination against them in the workplace.

Whatever system is in place for health care coverage, there must be parity between mental illnesses and other illnesses. This is essential. It should be mandated by the federal government, not left to the insurance industry to adopt voluntarily. Mental health advocates such as Rosalynn Carter have lobbied Congress for years on behalf of parity for coverage of mental health care, only to be thwarted.

Mrs. Carter is just as passionate in conversation about the importance of parity as she is when speaking about it in public. She distills the issue to its essence: It is unfair that people who suffer from mental illnesses receive less coverage from insurance than people who suffer from what are accepted as physical illnesses. More than 90 percent of insurance plans in this country discriminate against people with mental illness in ways that range from setting higher deductibles to refusing to pay for any treatment at all.

The failure to ensure parity for people suffering from mental illness is stigmatization on a grand scale. Mrs. Carter makes this point in her book *Helping Someone with Mental Illness*: "I have always believed that if insurance coverage made no distinction among illnesses, a lot of the stigma of the mental illnesses would fade away. The fact that they were covered would make them acceptable."

As Dr. Satcher insists, we must move affirmatively toward making the population of those who receive mental health care and those who provide it as racially and culturally diverse as the nation, with an emphasis on attracting more minority students to psychiatry courses in medical schools and psychiatry residencies after they graduate. Therapists can be trained to be sensitive to the needs of patients from varied cultural, racial, and ethnic backgrounds. My own experience as an African American male being treated by a white woman psychiatrist has been a good one, but I have no doubt that increasing the diversity of mental health care professionals will make mental health care more accessible and welcoming to a wider range of Americans.

All churches—and black churches, in particular—must become mental health resources. This would counter the way some in the church unintentionally reinforce the stigma of mental illness. The Stevie Wonder song "Have a Talk with God" illustrates my point: It promises that God will "give you peace of mind," and suggests that having a talk with Him will ease life's burdens. God, the song declares, is "the only free psychiatrist that's known throughout the world."

Without a doubt, the church and spirituality can be wonderful sources of inner strength. They have helped sustain African Americans throughout our history. They can and do help heal troubled minds. But it is patently wrong to ask people who are suffering to believe that religion is the only way out. And, finally, we cannot say that people who turn to their church and fail to find relief there have demonstrated that they lack faith or are morally weak.

Kenya Napper Bello told me how important spirituality was in helping her begin to heal after her husband Razak's suicide in 1994. Getting black churches involved is one of the primary goals of her crusade to increase awareness of mental illness and suicide among African American men. "I will speak about this in any church that will let me," she said. "The churches are so important in the black community. How could we *not* have them working on this problem?"

Fortunately, black churches are becoming more aware of the need to incorporate mental health care into pastoral counseling. I have met African American members of the clergy who realize that congregants who come to them suffering the pain of a mental illness need more than comfort and religious reassurances. They know that some people must be directed toward appropriate mental health treatment.

The Reverend Willie R. Rogers, Sr., a resident director at Morehouse College, is typical of such clergymen. "I'm hearing more and more ministers who say they want to help troubled members of their congregations who need more than prayer and counseling," he said. "That doesn't mean they don't ask God's help. They just understand that people also have to help themselves. Sometimes, when mental health problems are involved, helping people help themselves means guiding them to treatment."

I was raised a Southern Baptist, but I don't consider myself a religious person. My mother jokes that it has been so long since I regularly attended Sunday services that I think I have to knock on the church door before going in. Despite that, I believe strongly in the healing power of religious belief, in terms of both physical *and* mental health. Faith is an especially strong pillar of emotional well-being, I think. I've seen so many people whose faith forms the foundation for a positive outlook even in the bleakest circumstances.

I also have witnessed the way spirituality elevates people's mood in moments of great despair. There definitely can be a spiritual aspect to depression; in fact, one way of looking at depression is as a sickness of the spirit. And if there are no atheists in foxholes, there surely are few in the deepest hole of depression. The misery that depression visits upon people can make anyone call on God for help. Believing that there is a higher power to lift you out of depression certainly can have a therapeutic effect.

There was such a moment of spiritual therapy at the funeral of one of my uncles. The service moved along with the usual solemnity until my uncle's daughter-in-law came forward to sing a rousing solo of the gospel song "Going Up Yonder," backed by the church choir. In any other setting it would have been said that she brought the house down. But what she did with the song's rhythmic refrain of "I'm going up yonder to be with my Lord" was to lift the house and transform the funeral into a joyful celebration.

Even I, a man who might stand poised to rap on the church door before remembering that all are welcome to enter, can feel gospel music's mood-elevating power. There have been times when I wished I could bottle it. I seriously believe the music's potential as an antidepressant merits scientific study.

Speaking of studies, there have been many that claim better outcomes for patients who pray or know they are being prayed for. For example, a study reported in the December 2000 issue of the *Journal of Holistic Nursing* found that 96 percent of older adults use prayer to relieve stress. This study and others reporting similar results have been criticized for faulty methodology. But I understand why people feel that praying or being prayed for makes them feel better, both physically and emotionally. For religious people, prayer is a way of speaking to a God who listens to them. In His divine wisdom, He uses His power to make things right. People of faith know that prayers are not always answered, but prayers give them hope, and hope is what someone suffering from depression needs most.

Prayer can be good medicine even for nonbelievers. After I returned to work from my medical leave, a woman at the newspaper stopped me as I was leaving the cafeteria.

"Hi," she said. "It's good to see you back. I heard you were on sick leave. I hope you're feeling better."

"It was nothing serious," I lied. "There were just a few problems I had to take care of all at once."

"Well, I'm glad you're back," the woman said. "You know, I used to see you down here in the cafeteria, sitting by yourself and looking so sad. I thought there must be something troubling you. So I started praying for you. And when I heard you were out sick, I asked the members of my church to pray for you."

"Thank you," I said. "I am feeling better."

I was feeling better, and I felt a little better still knowing that someone who knew me only casually at work would care enough to include me in her prayers. That was a tonic for me.

A 1999 study by researchers at the Mid America Heart Institute in Kansas City asserts that praying for patients improves the outcome of their heart surgeries, even if the patients don't know they are being prayed for. Again, the methodology of the study and others like it has been disputed. Of course, the religious don't need scientific confirmation of what they believe. They rely on faith, which, as the Bible says, is belief in the substance of things hoped for, the evidence of things not seen.

Granted that religion can be a positive force in the lives of people with depression and those who care about them, the word "positive" is the key. Inherent in relying on religion is the danger of misinterpreting the meaning of the lack of a "cure." Some will believe that the person who doesn't get better with the assistance of prayer doesn't believe enough or is a bad person. That attitude is destructive and dangerous. It risks pushing the person with depression down to new depths rather than lifting him up. And the irony is that when religion is twisted in this way, the people suffering from depression who are most religious are done the most damage.

Promoting healthy minds should be a mission of every church. Institutions of worship have the capacity to carry out that mission, whether through music, counseling, or willingness to provide referral to professional help, or by other means. They only need the will and wisdom to use those tools.

I believe the steps I've outlined should be taken throughout the nation, not just in the African American community. But special steps should be taken to help black men deal with depression. Our society must devote adequate resources to research that will determine the true scope of the problem. We should acknowledge the high price being paid when the effects of black men's depression ripple through our families, our communities, and our nation.

We have to educate African American men and the people who care about them. Black men must know that depression can strike any of us. Whether we're languishing in the county jail or making deals in the corporate boardroom, any of us can be brought down by this disease. The myth of the emotionally invulnerable black man who can endure any pain in silence must be exploded. We must debunk the stereotype that violence is a natural impulse for troubled black men, so that any troubled black man must be dangerous. There are reasons why people behave in the ways they do. I believe depression may be a factor in the negative and destructive behavior of many black men. We ignore this at our peril.

The highest price we pay for our ignorance is the needless loss of lives. Before we can do something about the suicides of black men, we must do something about depression among black men. The latter leads to the former. If African American families and communities tolerate a youth culture in which death—especially violent death—is expected, accepted, and even glorified, the likelihood increases that depression will end in suicide. Young black men deserve reasons to live. We have to show them that their lives have value, and that society needs the contributions they can make. We must convince them that constantly imagining their own deaths, trying to show others that they have no fear of death, and reaching the point where they welcome death is not normal. It is a dire sign of a serious illness: depression.

There are lessons that even the most successful, accomplished African American men must learn to keep that illness from endangering their lives. The most important is that they should not be ashamed. I can understand why John Wilson, the chairman of the Washington, D.C., council, decided not to enter a mental hospital even though he knew that doing so might save his life. The stigma of mental illness could have ruined his political career. I wasn't a public figure like Wilson, yet I had some of the same concerns he had when I was trying to decide what to do about my depression. I feared my family, friends, and coworkers would think less of me. But I eventually came to fear my illness more than I feared revealing my illness. I decided to do whatever it took to get better, no matter what other people thought. It can be tough for anyone to come to such a realization. It's particularly difficult for black men, because of how our ideas about manhood and personal worth have been compromised and complicated by issues of race. Black men must be reassured that we will not be diminished in our communities if we suffer from depression.

In the end, however, African American men hold the key to releasing the chains of depression. Little else matters unless we have the courage to use that key. We must end our denial when the disease strikes us. We must end our refusal to seek and accept help in fighting it. We must end our silence. We must step out of the shadows of stigma and shame, into the light of acceptance and hope.

TEN

Finding Help and Reasons to Hope

All around me there's a solid wall.
A wall of trouble and confusion, I done tired of it all.
I believe, I believe I've been blue too long.

—B. B. King and Dave Clark,
"I Believe I've Been Blue Too Long"

It was the kind of fine spring evening that often blesses us in Atlanta. The light was brilliant even as it faded with the setting sun. The city's air was fresh and fragrant, as if filtered through the budding trees and new greenery before picking up the scent of blooming flowers. My mood was good. It wasn't just the weather that lifted my spirits. I drove to a restaurant to speak to the Atlanta chapter of the Chatauqua Society about my first book, *We Were the Land's: Biography of a Homeplace.* Most authors know the agony of going to a bookstore or library or anywhere else to set up a table to sell and sign books, only to sit and wonder whether anyone beyond your immediate family will show up. We also know the joy of being scheduled for a book event that comes with a guarantee that living, breathing, book-buying people will be there.

My audience that evening was a group of African American women who get together regularly to discuss books and other subjects of interest. Among those attending were some of the most successful women in Atlanta's history: a member of the Atlanta City

JOHN HEAD

Council, a newspaper publisher, attorneys, and others who have distinguished themselves in the city's businesses, politics, and civic affairs. Shirley Franklin was a late arrival. She had a good excuse. She was still busy getting her administration organized as the first woman elected mayor of Atlanta.

The discussion of *We Were the Land's* went well. The women seemed to relate to my memoir about my grandparents and their farm. Many had had similar experiences. They shared my feelings about family and place. Questions flowed; the discussion was lively.

Then someone asked if I was working on a sequel.

"No," I said. "I'm working on another book, but it's very different from this one. It's about black men and depression, and I'm writing about my own experiences as someone who suffered from depression for years before finally getting help."

There was a pause. For the briefest instant the room was filled with something that was like a silence but was not really a silence. The connection between the audience and me had changed. It had not been broken, but it had changed somehow. The questions still came, but they now had edges of intensity and, sometimes, urgency.

"What are the symptoms of depression?"

I spoke in general about the effects of the illness, including how it saps people's energy, causes them to lose interest in things that once gave them pleasure, and leaves them with an all-pervasive sense of hopelessness.

"Are black men at higher risk of depression?"

"The accepted statistics say we don't suffer depression at a significantly greater rate than the rest of the population," I said, "but I don't believe the statistics. I don't believe they're reliable because there hasn't been enough research on African American men and depression. I think there's more depression among black men than the experts say there is."

"What about black women?"

"There's actually been more research about depression and black women than there has been about depression and black men. I still

174

don't think there has been enough work done in this area, but there's some research indicating that, if you adjust for income, black women are less prone to depression than the general population. I think there's an idea out there that black people in general and black women in particular somehow can put up with more troubles than other people can and therefore are less likely to 'get depressed.' I definitely don't buy that." There were a few head nods and a whispered "Amen."

"Why won't black men talk about their depression?"

"For the same reasons that we won't talk about *anything* we're feeling," I replied.

"What made you get help?"

"I reached the point where I just couldn't go on without getting help," I said.

More questions along the same line followed. Finally, it was time to go. I signed a few copies of *We Were the Land's.* Several of the club members said they were looking forward to reading the next one.

As I waited for my car at valet parking, a woman walked up beside me. "I enjoyed your talk," she said. "I was especially interested in what you were saying about black men and depression. Do you mind if I ask you another question?"

"Sure," I said.

"How do you help someone with depression when they refuse to get any help?" she asked with obvious feeling. "What do you say to convince them? What can you do yourself to help them?"

"It's not easy," I said, and from that point on I mouthed things that probably were no better than babble. This woman had a problem that was affecting her deeply. I knew I wasn't going to come up with a solution in the time it took the valet to bring my car around. After I got into my car and drove away, I really worried that I had failed to say anything more useful to that woman than "It's not easy."

And I wondered about the other women at the meeting. All of them had been born with two strikes against them—being black and being women—yet they managed to live lives of achievement. But to judge by the questions they asked me, some of them were struggling with the idea that men they cared about might be suffering from depression, and they didn't know how to help.

Anyone trying to help a friend, a partner, or a relative deal with depression faces difficult dilemmas. However, there are things that can and should be done. There are approaches that can work. I know this from my research into depression and from living with depression. Here are some of the things beyond "It's not easy" I wish I had said to the woman who was looking for advice on that warm spring evening.

■ ■ ■

There are liable to be lots of barriers if you're trying to help an African American man get through depression. They include the same barriers anyone in this country might face: having no mental health care available; lacking access to the care that is available; not being able to afford that care. Generally, these barriers are bigger in the black community.

But, without doubt, the number one barrier to getting treatment for depression, the hurdle that's hardest to get over, is the stigma our society attaches to depression. Stigmatization keeps people from getting help when it is available, even when they can afford to pay for it or it is provided to them for free. The stigma is intensified in the black community. In the minds of black men, the stigma surrounding depression and mental health treatment creates a force field that can seem impossible to penetrate. It is the invisible wall between them and the help they need.

Depression can make a man feel that the more people try to help him, the less he wants their help. That certainly was my experience. As the illness worsens, this feeling intensifies. In the end, the decision to get help must come from inside us. We must be convinced of the necessity of it. We must believe that it will do some good. We must want it to do some good.

However, I believe our path to that point—the place where we realize that recovery is possible—is eased if people who care about us help us get there. They can be our lifelines. Their caring and support can help us survive as we wander through the wilderness of depression. But the best thing the people close to us can do for us is the most difficult: They can help us break through the stigma barrier. They can make us see that having depression is not a character flaw or a sign of any other weakness, and—most important of all—that needing professional help and getting it are nothing to be ashamed of.

The first step toward getting a black man to think about depression differently is to talk to him about it differently. Depression can bring on emotional and behavioral problems—mine fields for many men, and especially explosive mine fields for many African American men. We don't like to talk about our emotions. We are touchy in discussions about how we behave, either because we are ashamed when we behave badly (a shame heightened by the belief that such behavior confirms the worst stereotypes of black men) or because we believe the consequences of admitting to bad behavior will be particularly severe for a black man. Some of us believe that history and experience teach us that we don't "cop" to anything to anyone.

If you're trying to talk to a man about his depression and you're getting resistance, talk about the physical aspects of the illness. These mostly are neutral, nonjudgmental subjects, just as they would be in the context of any other physical ailment. Men may not want to hear advice about the emotional pain of depression. They don't mind hearing advice about getting a dentist to take a look at that aching tooth.

So, when talking about clinical depression, talk about the inability to sleep at night. Talk about fatigue during the day. Talk about other physical problems brought on by the disease. Suggest seeing a general practitioner about these symptoms. If, for example, you have a family doctor and you're able to get an appointment for your husband, family member, or friend, talk to the doctor in advance about any indications of depression—both physical and emotional—that you've observed. The doctor can sort out the symptoms. There is a push on in the medical profession for physicians in all fields to be alert for indications that their patients may have mental as well as physical problems. Many family doctors are familiar with the drugs that are helpful in dealing with depression. They also can offer referrals to mental health professionals. Taking this advice from a doctor may be easier for a man than taking the exact same advice from someone close to him.

Of course, many families don't have their own physician. Many don't see a doctor at all until there is an emergency. And many men won't see a doctor for any reason, much less reasons that have to do with depression. You have to keep communicating the idea that having depression is no different from having any other ailment. The person who is suffering from depression must be convinced that things *can* get better. Speak to him of being able to do the things he wants to do, if he gets treatment for this illness. A man who loves to play tennis knows that if he breaks his arm, he can't play until the broken arm is treated and healed. But if depression leaves the same man unable to drag himself out of bed to play the Saturday morning matches he has enjoyed for years, it may be harder for him to see—much less to admit—that he will regain his pleasure in the game if he treats the depression. The task of those who care about him is to encourage him to see the connection between what's going on in his mind and with his emotions—those areas that men too often refuse to explore themselves or allow others to look into—and how he's feeling and functioning physically.

Once he's ready, there are ways of finding help for the person you care about. Mental health advocates are working to make it easier for people to find providers, even in communities where mental health services aren't readily available. Organizations such as the National Mental Health Association have chapters in every state. These groups can provide referrals to therapists who are physically accessible to most communities. Local chapters of the American Medical Association can also provide information on mental health professionals. Mental health care providers are increasingly sensitive to the effects of cultural differences on which courses of treatment are most appropriate and effective. While San Francisco General Hospital's Black Focus Program may be one of a kind, the idea that African American men may have special needs while getting mental health care is gaining acceptance in the field. The priority should be getting each patient to the best practitioner. But a patient who's already reluctant to seek help certainly isn't going to see someone with whom he doesn't feel comfortable. An African American man may be most comfortable if the doctor is a man or black or both. This is an issue you should discuss with the man you're trying to help. Referring agencies probably will have the names of professionals who meet patients' preferences. Of course, the relatively small number of African American mental health care providers may make it more difficult to find one in some areas. Organizations such as the Black Psychiatrists of America may provide names that other agencies don't have.

As I've said, my own experience has been that a doctor's training and empathy are more important than gender, race, or cultural background. But such factors should not be ignored if they affect someone's willingness to seek professional help and to stick with treatment once it has begun.

If you have health insurance through your job, check to see whether mental health care is covered. If it is, you may still be limited to using therapists who participate in your company's plan. There also may be restrictions on what kind of therapist you can see and under what circumstances. For example, you could be required to get a referral from another physician before your insurance plan will pay for treatment by a psychiatrist.

Keep in mind that finding a therapist's name on your company's health insurance plan list of providers doesn't say anything about his or her ability to treat depression or any other mental illness. If there is an employee assistance program where you work, any list of therapists it maintains should at least be based on positive feedback from other employees who have seen the providers.

Anyone fortunate enough to have a choice of therapists should talk to the candidates to find a good match. Ask questions. Try to get a sense of how comfortable you can be with each one: The therapist-patient relationship will require mutual trust in order to achieve a good outcome.

State health departments have mental health divisions. These usually oversee a system of publicly funded mental health clinics in communities around the state. You shouldn't hesitate to take advantage of such resources.

It's unfortunate that so many African American men have their first contact with mental health care through the criminal justice system. Once they're in the custody of the state, the state is responsible for their health—including their mental health. If someone you care about winds up in this situation, make sure you know as much as possible about what his rights are and what the state is required to provide. Look into the quality of care. Again, advocacy groups are valuable resources. In recent years, many states have faced lawsuits over their lack of mental health services for inmates. A psychologist who works in Georgia's prison system—and who asked that I not use his name—told me that lawsuits, and the threat of lawsuits, are the only engines that push states to provide anything approaching adequate mental health services for prisoners. The records of these cases make it clear what the state must do. If it isn't done for each person in the state's custody, the state is subject to further legal sanctions. This is a tool you shouldn't be afraid to use if necessary.

If you're trying to help someone with depression, you may reach the point where you believe it's necessary to take steps to force the person to get treatment. This is one of the worst situations anyone can face. Involuntary commitment is not easily done, and for good reason. Your suspicion that someone is severely depressed is not enough, nor is a professional diagnosis of clinical depression alone. Most states require evidence that the person is a danger to himself or others.

Someone suffering from depression is much more likely to be a danger to himself than to others. If you are trying to help someone through depression and he shows signs that he might be suicidal, don't ignore the signs. A depressed man who says his family or friends would be better off without him is not attempting to be modest, noble, or selfless. He may be contemplating the unthinkable and asking as well as he can that someone step in and stop him. Such talk is a signal to get professional help as quickly as possible.

※ ※ ※

When a man's depression results in suicide, the suffering doesn't end, it's just transferred to the people who cared about him. Being a suicide survivor is difficult. The atmosphere of silence and denial that surrounds suicide in the African American community only makes the pain tougher to bear.

Earlier in this book, I mentioned Dr. Donna Barnes, the sociologist who is a founder and president of the National Organization of People of Color Against Suicide (NOPCAS). She devotes much of her time to helping African Americans who have been left behind when a family member or friend takes his own life. Her first student in suicide survival was herself.

In 1990, she was divorced, living in Boston, forty-two years old, and applying to law school. She wanted a degree that would allow her to teach business law at a university. Her twenty-year-old son, Marc Jamal Barnes, had moved from Texas to Boston to attend college on a baseball scholarship. He was a talented athlete. The Cincinnati Reds expressed interest in signing him to a contract, but his father insisted that he get his degree before trying pro ball.

Dr. Barnes thought her son was adjusting well to the move and to college, but on November 6 he disappeared from his dorm room. Earlier, his roommate had found him in the room, distraught. Marc said he wanted to kill himself. He gave the roommate a note that said, "Tell my mom I love her. Tell my dad I love him. Tell my sister I love her." Telling Marc he had to go to the bathroom, the roommate went looking for help. He was gone for only seven minutes, but when he returned, Marc was gone.

"I had nine months to prepare for my son's birth," Dr. Barnes told me. "I had seven months to prepare for his death."

Seven months. That's how long it took to find Marc Jamal Barnes's body. He had driven his car into Boston's Merrimack River. When all hope that her son might be alive finally was gone, Donna Barnes began trying to cope with his suicide.

"I started reading everything I could get my hands on about suicide," she said. "I told myself that I shouldn't do all this reading for nothing, so I switched to sociology. Every paper I wrote was about suicide. My advisers finally got sick of it. They said I should write about something else—anything else. By then I think I had written fifteen papers about suicide. And then my dissertation was on suicide survivors among African Americans."

All the while, she was doing what many people say you shouldn't do in the wake of a suicide: She was asking herself why Marc had killed himself.

"When someone does that, it's like someone getting up and leaving the room and not saying anything, and without even saying good-bye," she said. "You want to ask, 'Why, why, why?' It's a natural question. It's a legitimate question. I think people should ask it."

The answer Dr. Barnes came up with was that her son was hurting over several things, including his parents' divorce and having to move with his mother from Texas to Boston. He was depressed and he didn't know how to talk about it. "He was like most men," she said. "Men are about internalizing their pain. They're not socialized like women are. They aren't socialized to show their emotions."

Answering the why wasn't enough, though. Donna Barnes needed more. She began going to meetings of support groups for suicide survivors. She found them very helpful, but there was something about them that nagged her. "At survivor conferences I noticed I was the only one integrating the meeting. I knew about the increasing suicide rate among African Americans. I looked around and asked myself, 'Where are all the other black people?'"

When she traveled to a conference in Washington, D.C., she figured there would be plenty of African Americans at a meeting in that majority-black city. "There were three others there besides me. This happened again and again. I went to conferences and there would be only one or two other black people. And most of the time they were complaining about the support groups, saying, 'They're not doing anything for black people. They're not integrating enough. They don't care about the African American community.' My answer was to ask, 'Why don't we do it for ourselves?' It was important for us to go out into the community and let people know that suicide is not a 'white thing.' "

Donna Barnes's activism in response to her son's suicide began to get notice. The *Boston Globe* newspaper did a front-page article on her. "That article changed my life," she said. "A woman in Teaneck, New Jersey, read it on the day of her son's suicide. She called me. She called me back when another child killed himself. Within a few months, she told me about four suicides of kids in Teaneck's African American community. We decided to organize a conference for Teaneck."

Doris Smith of Atlanta and Les Franklin of Denver, two other African American parents who have lost sons to suicide, traveled to Teaneck with Dr. Barnes. They set up a meeting room for fifteen people, hoping they would attract about ten. It turned out to be standing room only when thirty-five showed up. "We introduced ourselves and told our stories," she said. "That's how we got started." It was 1998, and the National Organization of People of Color Against Suicide (NOPCAS) was born.

I asked Dr. Barnes whether she believed attitudes toward suicide in the African American community made it more difficult for suicide survivors. She said she thought so. So what do you tell people to help them cope? I asked.

"There are all sorts of coping strategies," she said. "First of all, you have to tell people about it. I told everyone. I walked into the convenience store and the clerk said, 'Hi. How are you?' I said, 'My son killed himself.' He just looked at me. He didn't know what to say. Fortunately, some more customers came in and he could just get busy with them.

"It was difficult for me, but I had to talk about it. I was divorced. Whenever I went on a date, I wondered how I would tell the person that my son killed himself. I didn't go out with someone unless I felt comfortable talking with him about it. If I told someone about it and he acted as if he wasn't comfortable with that, I didn't go out with him again.

"Coping is an individual thing. You can't say put A plus B [together] and this is how you cope. Some people don't like support groups. The first support group I went to was so draining, but I couldn't wait to go to the next meeting. I felt so relieved to finally let all that pent-up stuff out.

"I tell people it's important to go through the grieving process. It's very important. As African Americans we don't know how to do that. We're all about getting on with our lives. We don't allow ourselves to grieve."

Do you tell people not to feel guilty about someone's suicide? I asked.

"Oh, no," she said. "Guilt. That's a very normal reaction. I tell people to just go with that. You can't tell a parent not to feel guilty about their child's suicide. You go with that, you question that. You do that until you understand that it isn't your fault."

It's not possible for all those who lose loved ones to suicide to turn their personal tragedies into public crusades the way Dr. Donna Barnes and Kenya Napper Bello have. These two women have tremendous courage and capacity for caring. But if their efforts to save others earn our admiration, it is the determination they showed in saving themselves that should serve as suicide survivors' inspiration. They refused to be destroyed by their losses. Kenya Bello told me how a heightened spirituality allowed her to experience her grief fully without giving in to it completely. Whatever the source they draw it from, those left behind by suicide have to find their own strength eventually.

■　■　■

Don't blame yourself.

That's essential advice if you're trying to help someone close to you who is suffering from depression. Too many people do blame themselves. This is especially true of women dealing with men they love. They believe they are the cause of the depression. They expect they can be the cure. Neither of these things is true.

A person with clinical depression suffers from an illness of the brain that is no different from other diseases that afflict the body. The people close to someone with depression don't cause the illness any more than the people close to someone with kidney disease or asthma cause that person to be sick. And none of those illnesses— not kidney disease, not asthma, not depression, not any other dis-ease—will be cured merely because the people around the sufferer start to behave differently.

Clinical depression affects the mind's ability to function, just as other illnesses affect the body's ability to function. In someone suffering from asthma, for example, the lungs are not able to handle physical exertion as efficiently as the lungs of someone who doesn't have asthma. In the same way, the mind of someone with depression is not able to handle emotional exertion—sadness or stress, for example—as the mind of someone who is not suffering from depression. Being nice to someone with asthma may make him feel better emotionally, but it won't cure his physical ailment. This is what is doubly insidious about depression: Not only may trying to help someone with the disease fail to cure him, it may actually make him feel worse emotionally, because of a sense of guilt for not being able to respond appreciatively or even positively to those who offer help.

These things are easy to say, but difficult to accept for anyone trying to help a loved one get through clinical depression. Because the symptoms of the illness are most obvious in someone's emotional outlook, it is difficult for the people at the center of the depressed person's emotional life to separate themselves from what causes the illness. The person most likely to be at the center of a man's emotional life is a woman, so a woman is most likely to take on the blame and to become a victim of depression's toxic by-products.

In fact, the hurt a man with depression feels has a way of radiating to the people around him, as the Surgeon General's Report on Mental Health points out: "Spouses, children, parents, siblings, and friends experience frustration, guilt, anger, financial hardship, and, on occasion, physical abuse in their attempts to assuage or cope with the depressed person's suffering."

In blaming yourself for someone's depression and believing that it's your job to end his depression, you do no good for the person who is suffering and you may do yourself harm. If you believe the man in your life has depression, be supportive, encourage him to seek help, do all that you can to get help for him. But don't bring unnecessary anguish and anxiety on yourself by believing that his depression begins and ends with you.

Once you're beyond the blame game, there's another hurdle to overcome. That's the temptation to believe that depression explains everything that's wrong with your relationship with the person who is suffering from depression. This is especially true when African American men and women are involved: Societal stereotypes and our cultural history create domestic dynamics that are laced with dread for us. There are expectations that African American men will engage in destructive behaviors. As unfair as it is to apply such expectations to all black men, the characterization isn't made up out of whole cloth. Too many young black men help bring children into the world and then shirk their duty to help support them. Too many black men abandon their families. Too many mistreat the women in their lives.

I said earlier that depression may well play a role in some of these behaviors. But while depression may help explain bad behavior, it does not excuse it. Depression can take a great deal from us, but it does not rob us of our moral compass. It may sap our energy to do a lot of things, but it does not leave us unable to see what's the right thing to do.

My own experience has been that depression interferes with my ability to be the kind of father my three sons deserve. Sometimes it denies me the simple pleasures I should get from doing things with them. Sometimes it makes me yearn for passivity and solitude when I could spend time with them. The worst of it, of course, is that if depression grips me this way, my sons see what's happening from their perspective. They see that Dad isn't enjoying himself with them. They see that there are times when Dad doesn't want to spend time with them at all.

I love my sons. I want them to know that I love them; I want to show them that I love them. My love for them is one of the main reasons I finally decided to do something about my depression. I didn't want history to be repeated. I didn't want them to be denied a father the way I was. And even if I didn't desert my family the way my father did his, my sons could have felt the absence of the father they needed. They would have been denied him by depression instead of by distance. In fact, when I was in the throes of depression, I really believed my sons would be better off if I weren't there.

My desire to be a good father to my sons motivates me to face up to my depression and do what I must do to fight it. Getting help gives me the energy to do things with them and to take pleasure in doing them. I experience joy teaching them sports, watching them compete for their school teams, attending their music and acting performances, going fishing with them, taking them to the movies, working with them down on the farm . . . on and on. Most people would see these as simple acts that are the basics of fatherhood. But even if a father wants to participate in his children's lives, his depression can keep it from happening. I refuse to let my depression keep those simple joys from me and my sons.

When a man's depression contributes to irresponsible behavior or family dysfunction, the solution has to include dealing with the depression. Healing can't begin without taking that step; without that step, there is no hope. But always remember my earlier cautionary note: The idea that depression explains everything is much too simplistic. While it's true that men who really want to be good fathers can suffer from depression, so do men who have no interest in being good fathers. In both cases, the depression should be confronted. It's just that in the former case, the healing begins with the man and then spreads to the people around him because he intends to do the right thing. In the latter, there may be healing for the man who has suffered, but it stops with him. He still has no intention of living up to his responsibilities. He is not willing to be the father his children deserve. Even if he conquers his depression, he still has a lot of work to do. Depression doesn't only happen to good people; it also happens to bad people, who will continue to be bad when the depression is dealt with—unless other changes are made.

I don't want to take away any shred of hope from someone who's close to a depressed man. That person has to believe that things will get better if the depression is treated, and has to know that they are likely to get worse if it is not. But to believe that depression does explain everything really can lead to frustration, heartache, and even danger. For example, depression can lead to problems with anger management. But no one should see depression as an explanation—much less an excuse—for domestic violence.

No matter how much you care about someone with depression, no matter how strongly you believe he will be a happier, healthier person if he gets treatment for the illness, if there is violence in the relationship, your first order of business is to stop being a victim of the violence. In doing that, you have to accept the truth that just as it is unlikely that depression is the sole cause of the violence, so treating the depression doesn't guarantee an end to the violence.

In the last few pages, I've said a lot about what *not* to do when someone close to you suffers from depression and you want to do everything you can to help him get better. Saying those things is important because I've experienced how my depression hurt the people around me. Depression impaired my ability to make decisions that affected me and affected people I care deeply about. With my mind clouded by the belief that my choices would never lead to happiness, I made some bad decisions. But looking back, I wish I had done more to protect the people I love, and that they had done more to protect themselves.

Even while protecting yourself and making sure that your expectations are realistic, there are ways to be a positive force in the recovery of someone you care about. By its nature, depression can make it appear that every possible path out of the maze leads to a dead end. This pessimism can envelop the depressed person *and* those who are trying to help him.

Healing is possible. People can be put on the path to recovery even if they start the journey with little information and few resources. I found proof of this in the story of Vernell Garrett and her family. I met her late in 1999, on the eve of the release of the Surgeon General's Report on Mental Health. I wanted to write about ordinary Georgians who had been affected by mental health problems. Vernell Garrett certainly fit the bill. For years, she struggled as a single black mother confronting the emotional turmoil that swirled around her and her children, especially her son, Robert. During much of that time, she got little or no help. But she refused to give up.

"When it first started, all I would see at home was crying," Garrett told me, referring to her son's behavior when he was in grade school. "Robert would literally scream at the top of his voice for hours."

The child seemed unable to control his emotions. The outbursts mostly seemed to be the self-directed venting of frustration. But one day, when Robert was nine years old, something happened that made Varnell Garrett fear that her son might be dangerous. Robert was arguing with a neighbor's child. Suddenly, he picked her up and seemed poised to throw her over an apartment balcony.

"I screamed, and he put her down," Garrett recalled. "He went in the house, locked himself in the bedroom, and proceeded to tear the bedroom up. By the time I got in the door the bed was turned over, the dresser was turned over. There was a toy truck he had thrown with so much force that it was literally sticking out of the wall.

"I didn't know what he was going to do, so I wrestled and tussled with him on the floor, trying to hold him down," Garrett said. This was not as easy as it may sound. Robert eventually grew to be six foot four and three hundred pounds. At nine, he already was almost as big as his mother. "All of a sudden he just went to sleep in the middle of the tussle," Garrett continued. "Just fell sound asleep."

The incident convinced Garrett that her son needed help beyond anything she could give him alone. She quit her job as a day-care worker to devote as much time as possible to dealing with Robert's problems. Her first efforts involved the counselors at the public schools and alternative schools that Robert was shuttled among as a result of disciplinary problems. Garrett says the counselors weren't very helpful. They told her Robert was basically a bad kid who threw tantrums. She thought most of them saw him as a "typical" young black male, prone to acting out violently. Some even told Garrett that *she* was the problem, because she lacked the parenting skills that were required of a single mom trying to cope with two children.

Things didn't start to change until, at age eleven, Robert was put in the juvenile justice system after striking a teacher. Sue Smith, director of the Georgia Parent Support Network, began working with the family. Smith's group works to provide children access to mental health services. The juvenile court judge who heard Robert's case ordered a full psychiatric evaluation for him. Major depression was among the diagnoses that therapists reached.

Sue Smith told me it was good luck that Robert came before a judge who was willing to search for the reason behind bad behavior rather than lock a child up. In 1999, eight years after that juvenile court judge decided to dig deeper into Robert's problems, more judges in Georgia preferred treatment over punishment, but problems persisted. "Things are better today," Smith said, "but still, the need for mental health services far exceeds what the system offers."

Vernell Garrett says her son is basically a gentle giant when he takes the medications prescribed for him. But Robert, who was nineteen when I spoke to him, didn't like the medicines' numbing side effects. "All the medications make me sleepy," Robert told me. "All of it. I would just sit like a couch potato."

Robert came across to me as very thoughtful. He was articulate, measuring his words carefully. His attitude toward psychotropic drugs reflects the view among many blacks—a view that, I believe, makes it more difficult to begin taking such medications and to continue the regimen once it has begun. Many of us distrust the idea that drugs can improve our emotional state; that concept seems not far removed from reasons people take the illegal drugs that are destroying our communities. People start using crack or heroin or whatever because they believe it will make them feel better emotionally. Eventually, they *have* to take the drug to "feel better," to escape being the person they've become. That's the way Robert came to see the antidepressants he was supposed to take. He is willing to continue sessions with a therapist, believing that talking about his problems helps him to see what he's doing wrong and to take responsibility for it. But he refuses to believe that medicine will "cure" him. "I'm a firm believer that people don't change unless they want to change," he said. "I believe medication doesn't change a person."

So Robert has had a cycle of going on and off his medications. His mother says that when he's on his medication for intermittent explosive disorder—which is characterized by sudden rages—he's able to control his temper and hold down a job. When he goes off the medication, he loses his job and has run-ins with the law. Still, she believes he is better off than he would have been had he not started getting treatment. At least she knows, and he knows, that there are ways of making things better for him. Vernell Garrett became a mental health advocate for her son. She urges him to stay on his medication. When he has wound up in jail, she has told authorities about his mental health problems and has tried to see that he has access to whatever treatment is available. As bad as things can get for Robert as a result of his depression, they could be much worse were it not for his mother's persistence and her refusal to accept the idea that her son's behavior is nothing more than should be expected from a young black male.

Despite lacking information, money, a support system, and other invaluable resources, Vernell Garrett achieved a measure of success in dealing with Robert's depression. However, success isn't always possible, even for those who are blessed with all the resources Vernell Garrett didn't have.

As with everything else in life, there are no guarantees. Examples abound of cases in which people tried to help but couldn't do enough. Razak Bello had his wife, Kenya, a smart and caring woman who loved him and wanted to give him reasons to believe in himself so they could live the rest of their lives together the way they had planned. The Washington, D.C., council president, John Wilson, also had a loving wife. He was surrounded by people who understood what he was going through and gave him excellent advice about what to do about it. Yet depression killed both men.

The fact remains, however, that the chances of reaching the point of healing are increased for any man who has people who care about him and are willing to take on the difficult task of breaking through all the barriers between him and getting help. That's what he needs. He needs someone who cares about him and loves him enough to offer help when it seems that all he gives in return is resistance and resentment. Your willingness to help him find his way to his own decision to seek help, to find that place within himself where there remains a spark of hope, can mean the difference between illness and recovery.

It can mean the difference between life and death.

ELEVEN

A Guide to Resources for Fighting Depression

If you are a black man fighting depression, the first objective is to gain some measure of control over the illness. That control is born out of knowledge, whether it's knowledge gained on your own or with help from people who care about you. Two formidable barriers stand between African American men and the information essential to understanding and overcoming depression. First and foremost is our reluctance to believe we need information about depression. "Why learn about something that doesn't affect us?" we ask ourselves. The second hurdle is our lack of a cultural database about depression—a collection of common knowledge we might call upon if mental illness was not such a taboo topic in our communities.

I found these and other lesser obstacles could be overcome once I decided to be an active participant in my own recovery. I armed myself with information, borrowing from whatever arsenals were open to me. My Carter Center fellowship—by allowing me to attend conferences and seminars on mental health and giving me entrée to top researchers and practitioners in the field—provided me with high-caliber ammunition. However, most of what I needed is available to anyone willing to look in the right places. This chapter offers guidance on how to do just that.

Dealing with depression requires a diagnosis of the disease. Early in this book I describe the symptoms of clinical depression. The description includes a summary of criteria the American Psychiatric Association's *Diagnostic and Statistical Manual of Mental Disorders*, Fourth Edition (DSM-IV), lists for major depressive disorder. Here is the complete list of symptoms. It provides a clearer picture and deeper understanding of what major depression is.

According to the DSM-IV, an episode of major depressive disorder may be diagnosed when:

A. Five (or more) of the following symptoms have been present during the same 2-week period and represent a change from previous functioning; at least one of the symptoms is either (1) depressed mood or (2) loss of interest or pleasure.

Note: Do not include symptoms that are clearly due to a general medical condition, or mood-incongruent delusions or hallucinations.

1. depressed mood most of the day, nearly every day, as indicated by either subjective report (e.g., feels sad or empty) or observation made by others (e.g., appears tearful). **Note:** In children and adolescents, can be irritable mood.
2. markedly diminished interest or pleasure in all, or almost all, activities most of the day, nearly every day (as indicated by either subjective account or observation made by others).
3. significant weight loss when not dieting or weight gain (e.g., a change of more than 5% of body weight in a month), or decrease or increase in appetite nearly every day. **Note:** In children, consider failure to make expected weight gains.
4. insomnia or hypersomnia nearly every day.
5. psychomotor agitation or retardation nearly every day (observation by others, not merely subjective feelings or restlessness or being slowed down).
6. fatigue or loss of energy nearly every day.

7. feelings of worthlessness or excessive or inappropriate guilt (which may be delusional) nearly every day (not merely self-reproach or guilt about being sick).
8. diminished ability to think or concentrate, or indecisiveness, nearly every day (either subjective account or as observed by others).
9. recurrent thoughts of death (not just fear of dying), recurrent suicidal ideation without a specific plan, or a suicide attempt or a specific plan for committing suicide.

B. The symptoms do not meet criteria for a mixed episode.
C. The symptoms cause clinically significant distress or impairment in social, occupational, or other important areas of functioning.
D. The symptoms are not due to the direct physiological effects of a substance (e.g., a drug of abuse, a medication) or a general medical condition (e.g., hypothyroidism).
E. The symptoms are not better accounted for by bereavement, i.e., after loss of a loved one; the symptoms persist for longer than 2 months or are characterized by marked functional impairment, morbid preoccupation with worthlessness, suicidal ideation, psychotic symptoms, or psychomotor retardation.

The DSM-IV also describes diagnostic criteria for "dysthymic disorder," a chronic form of depression that can strike early in childhood and last a lifetime if left untreated. The symptoms are listed as follows:

A. Depressed mood for most of the day, for more days than not, as indicated either by subjective account or observation by others, for at least 2 years.

Note: In children and adolescents, mood can be irritable and duration must be at least 1 year.

B. Presence, while depressed, of two (or more) of the following:

1. poor appetite or overeating
2. insomnia or hypersomnia
3. low energy or fatigue
4. low self-esteem
5. poor concentration or difficulty making decisions
6. feelings of hopelessness

C. During the 2-year period (1 year for children or adolescents) of the disturbance, the person has never been without the symptoms in Criteria A and B for more than 2 months at a time.

D. No major depressive episode has been present during the first 2 years of the disturbance (1 year for children and adolescents); i.e., the disturbance is not better accounted for by chronic major depressive disorder, or major depressive disorder, in partial remission.

Note: There may have been a previous major depressive episode provided there was a full remission (no significant signs or symptoms for 2 months) before development of the dysthymic disorder. In addition, after the initial 2 years (1 year in children or adolescents) of dysthymic disorder, there may be superimposed episodes of major depressive disorder, in which case both diagnoses may be given when the criteria are met for a major depressive episode.

E. There has never been a manic episode, a mixed episode, or a hypomanic episode, and criteria have never been met for cyclothymic disorder.

F. The disturbance does not occur exclusively during the course of a chronic psychotic disorder, such as schizophrenia or delusional disorder.

G. The symptoms are not due to the direct physiological effects of a substance (e.g., a drug of abuse, a medication) or a general medical condition (e.g., hypothyroidism).

H. The symptoms cause clinically significant distress or impairment in social, occupational, or other important areas of functioning.

As these criteria make clear, arriving at a diagnosis of depression requires more than checking off items from the lists. A diagnosis depends to a great degree on how we see ourselves (the "subjective report" mentioned in the DSM-IV) or how others see us (the "observation made by others"). For African Americans—and especially for African American men—these perceptions are complicated by our history, by our culture, and by our place in American society. Simply put, we are bombarded with the idea that hopelessness, low self-esteem, indecisiveness, recurrent thoughts of death, and other negative emotional states are our lot in life, not symptoms of a disease. We become convinced that a black man in America really is born to have the blues.

That kind of thinking is dangerous. It puts us on the path to depression's worst outcome—suicide. Severe depression is a primary risk factor for suicide. Once you identify symptoms of depression in yourself or others, it's time to watch for the warning signs of suicide. The reasons why people wind up taking their own lives can be very complex. These may be influenced by factors such as age, gender, and cultural background. There's no such thing as a "typical suicide." Rarely does someone just snap under pressure and kill himself in a spur-of-the-moment decision. The road to self-killing most often is long, twisted, and tortured.

Even though people reach the point of suicide for many different reasons, there are behaviors that frequently precede suicide. In addition to symptoms of serious depression, here are warning signs to watch for:

- A previous suicide attempt. Never brush off a suicide attempt—no matter how inept—as nothing more than "attention-getting" behavior. Even someone who goes through the motions and stops short of suicide is at higher risk of completing the act in the future.

- Talk of suicide. A man who says things like, "If I had any courage, I'd kill myself" or, "The world would be a better place without me" or, "You would be better off with me dead" or, "What's the use of living if things will never change?" should be taken seriously.

- Unusually reckless and self-destructive behavior, such as speeding and abuse of alcohol.

- A sudden obsession with tying up loose ends and getting one's affairs in order, such as writing wills and meeting long-standing obligations.

- An abrupt decision to give away possessions with high personal value, such as a pet, or to quit a job or to go on a spending spree that drains finances.

- Self-imposed isolation from others, including family and friends.

If you see someone exhibiting these kinds of behaviors, talk to him as directly as possible. This is not the time for embarrassment. Ask him if he's thinking of killing or hurting himself. Talk about the consequences of what he might do. Tell him how worried you are. As I said earlier, urge him to get help.

CHOOSING THE RIGHT TREATMENT

By the time I finally decided to get help with my depression, I was in no condition to be choosy about the kind of treatment I received.

My illness had reached the crisis point. The priority was to do whatever brought me back to emotional stability as quickly as possible. That's the way it is for many black men suffering from depression. We don't take action until we have to or are forced to. Even so, unless we enter treatment under the direst circumstances—such as winding up behind bars or in a homeless shelter—we do have options from which to choose.

The first choice is who you go to for help. Talking about depression can be therapeutic in and of itself. If you can put what you are feeling into words, you may gain insights into and a fresh perspective on your situation. This can be a major step forward, and all you need to accomplish it is a sympathetic ear. That ear might belong a loved one, a friend, a pastor—to anyone willing to listen.

Of course, if merely talking about depression were enough, we could all cure ourselves. Dealing with major depression requires more. The involvement of someone trained to treat the illness is essential.

There is a broad range of mental health practitioners available. They are differentiated by various factors, from which therapeutic methods they employ to what services the law allows them to provide.

Following are brief descriptions of some the most commonly available mental health care providers. This list does not cover all the categories, nor does it account for the disciplines within these categories.

Clinical social workers are trained in the prevention, diagnosis, and treatment of mental, behavioral, and emotional disorders. Licensing requirements may vary from state to state, but clinical social workers must have a master's degree or a doctorate in social work, followed by supervised clinical experience.

Psychologists must have a doctorate, usually earned in four to six years of graduate study of mental health. They also serve a supervised internship. They may be trained as clinicians or researchers.

Psychiatrists are physicians who spend three-year residencies in mental health training after they've completed medical school and internships. They are the only mental health clinicians authorized to prescribe medications.

Psychoanalysts, who may have various advanced degrees, are distinguished from other mental health professionals by an additional six to ten years of training in psychoanalysis. They must undergo analysis themselves, and at the end of their training, they conduct psychoanalysis of patients under the supervision of experienced analysts. Psychoanalysis is sometimes called "the talking cure" because of the way discussion with the therapist delves into the patient's subconscious to find the roots of emotional problems.

Of course, a black man seeking treatment for depression may find limited options when it comes to choosing a therapist. Who is available and who is affordable can become crucial factors. Location alone can make a huge difference. For example, a community near a university with a postdoctoral clinical psychology program may offer access to low-cost care by postdocs supervised by experienced clinicians. Some might see this as compromising on quality of care, but it can be a good introduction to treatment.

Starting treatment with a therapist whose training meets your needs and with whom you feel comfortable is the key to a successful outcome.

OTHER BOOKS ON DEPRESSION

Information on depression is plentiful. I've found that only a small fraction of that information is specifically about and for black men with depression. General knowledge about the disease is essential. Here are some books that I believe provide helpful information.

The first book I read about depression was Kay Redfield Jamison's *An Unquiet Mind: A Memoir of Moods and Madness*. It is a lyrically written, informative book. I also highly recommend Jamison's *Night Falls Fast: Understanding Suicide*.

Lay My Burden Down: Unraveling Suicide and the Mental Health Crisis among African-Americans is an excellent book. Written by Harvard psychiatrist Alvin F. Poussaint and Amy Alexander, it delves into the issues of suicide and mental illness in the black community as has not been done before.

Anyone trying to figure out what to do for someone with depression will find that Rosalynn Carter's *Helping Someone with Mental Illness: A Compassionate Guide for Family, Friends, and Caregivers* is a source of information and inspiration.

The Noonday Demon: An Atlas of Depression by Andrew Solomon is a comprehensive and highly readable look at many aspects of depression.

Psychiatrist David D. Burns's *Feeling Good: The New Mood Therapy* offers advice on self-treatment of depression through cognitive therapy.

This brief list barely scratches the surface of literature about depression. Visit a bookstore or library and look for titles that appeal to you.

ORGANIZATIONS THAT CAN HELP

As with every other subject, the Internet seems to be a limitless source of information on depression. While it's true that the more knowledge we gain about depression the better off we are, having all that information swirling about in the electronic ether isn't all good. Some of what's out there is bound to be misinformation—confusing, misleading, or just plain wrong. The best way to vet information is to get it from a reputable source. Here are some of the organizations I've found to be reliable sources of information on depression and related issues. Again, this is only a partial list of the many organizations that offer information, advice, and help with depression. Contact information—including website addresses—is provided below.

Organizations of Special Interest to African Americans

Association of Black Psychologists
P.O. Box 55999
Washington, DC 20040-5999
202-722-0808
www.abpsi.org

Black Psychiatrists of America
c/o Dr. Angela Shannon-Reid, Treasurer
5050 Montcalm Drive
Atlanta, GA 30333
www.blackpsychiatristsofamerica.com

Health Power, Incorporated
(a source for minority health information)
3020 Glenwood Road
Brooklyn, NY 11210
718-434-8103
www.healthpoweronline.org

National Association of Black Social Workers
1220 11th Street NW
Washington, DC 20001
202-589-1850
www.nabsw.org

National Center for Primary Care
Morehouse School of Medicine
720 Westview Drive SW

Atlanta, GA 30310
404-756-5740
www.msm.edu/ncpc.htm

National Medical Association
(America's oldest association of black physicians)
1012 Tenth Street, NW
Washington, DC 20001
202-347-1895
www.nmanet.org

National Organization of People of Color Against Suicide
4715 Sargent Road, NE
Washington, DC 20017
866-899-5317
www.nopcas.com

Other Organizations

American Association of Pastoral Counselors
9504A Lee Highway
Fairfax, VA 22031
703-385-6967
www.aapc.org

American Counseling Association
5999 Stevenson Avenue
Alexandria, VA 22304
800-347-6647
www.counseling.org

American Medical Association
515 North State Street
Chicago, IL 60610
800-621-8335
www.ama-assn.org

American Mental Health Counselors Association
801 North Fairfax Street, Suite 304
Alexandria, VA 22314
800-326-2642
www.amhca.org

American Psychiatric Association
1000 Wilson Boulevard, Suite 1825
Arlington, VA 22209-3901
703-907-7300
www.psych.org

American Psychoanalytic Association
309 East 49th Street, #4P
New York, NY 10017
212-752-0450
www.apsa.org

American Psychological Association
750 First Street, NE
Washington, DC 20002-4242
800-374-2721
www.apa.org

Carter Center Mental Health Program
453 Freedom Parkway
Atlanta, GA 30307
404-420-5165
www.cartercenter.org

Depression and Bipolar Support Alliance
730 North Franklin, Suite 501
Chicago, IL 60134
800-826-3632
www.dbsalliance.org

National Alliance for the Mentally Ill
Colonial Place Three
2107 Wilson Boulevard, Suite 300
Arlington, VA 22201
800-950-6264
www.nami.org

National Association of Social Workers
750 First Street, NE, Suite 700
Washington, DC 20002-4241
202-408-8600
www.socialworkers.org

National Institute of Mental Health
Office or Communications
6001 Executive Boulevard
Room 8184, MSC 9663
Bethesda, MD 20892-9663
800-615-6464
www.nimh.nih.gov

National Mental Health Association
2001 North Beauregard Street, 12th Floor
Alexandria, VA 22311-1732
703-684-7722
www.nmha.org

**Substance Abuse and Mental Health
Services Administration**
Room 12–105, Parklawn Building
5600 Fishers Lane
Rockville, MD 20857
301-443-4795
www.samhsa.gov

Suicide Prevention Action Network USA
1025 Vermont Avenue NW, Suite 1200
Washington, DC 20005
202-449-3600
www.spanusa.org

The Surgeon General of the United States
Office of the Surgeon General
Room 18–66
5600 Fishers Lane
Rockville, MD 20857
301-443-4000
www.surgeongeneral.gov

ACKNOWLEDGMENTS

In the fall of 2000, I had an opportunity most writers can only dream of. I sat in the office of the president of a publishing company and explained my proposal to write a book about black men and depression. He listened patiently. When I was done, he had a question.

"Depressed people don't really read much, do they?" he asked.

I should have offered a snappy comeback about marketing the book to those of us with bipolar tendencies during our manic phases. That would sell lots of copies. Instead, I left the office wondering if I would find anyone who believed in my book.

Well, it wasn't long before I found someone who did. Her name is Beth Vesel. She became my literary agent, and she is the person who deserves the most credit for getting this work published. Beth's book business savvy and connections, her passion for and knowledge of mental health issues, and her incredible work ethic made her the perfect person to represent this book. She has been both ardent advocate and wise adviser. My debt to her cannot be adequately accounted in the space allotted here.

There would have been no book to champion without the Rosalynn Carter Mental Health Journalism Fellowship Program at the Jimmy Carter Presidential Center. Work on this book began there. Mrs. Carter is the driving force behind the program. As she does with all the fellows, she took the time to personally encourage and support me in my work. She is, indeed, the First Lady of mental health in America. Mrs. Carter is my hero.

ACKNOWLEDGMENTS

The leaders and staff of the Carter Center Mental Health Program provided invaluable assistance during my fellowship. Dr. Greg Fricchione, the program's director when my year began, and Dr. Thomas Bornemann, his successor in that job, gave me more of their time and attention than their busy schedules should have allowed. Lei Ellingson, Rebecca Palpant, Lynne Randolph, and Valrie Thompson also went above and beyond their duties to provide any help I needed. They have never let me down.

Beth Vesel promised to find not just a publishing house for my book but a publishing home—a place where people would care about the book and treat it and me with respect. She found that place at Broadway Books. I was fortunate that Vice President and Executive Editor Janet Hill agreed to serve as editor for this book. Her sensitivities and insights into mental health issues in general and African Americans in particular were beacons that guided me. She has the light touch and steady hand every writer would wish for in an editor. Tracy Jacobs, Janet's assistant, helped me navigate the administrative details of the publishing process, pushing me to fulfill various duties and meet deadlines in a way that always felt like gentle encouragement. Finally, I appreciate the work of the copyeditor, Jolanta Benal. The thoroughness and thoughtfulness of the questions she raised and the changes she suggested made this a better book than it would have been otherwise.

I am not an expert on mental health; this book is not written from an expert's perspective. But my Carter Center fellowship opened doors to conferences on mental health and gave me entrée to experts and researchers. Some of those people are quoted in the book. Others who provided information and guidance are too numerous to mention. However, I must give special thanks to Vanessa Jackson for allowing me to use her manuscript "In Our Own Voice: African-American Stories of Oppression, Survival and Recovery in Mental Health Systems" as a resource. Vanessa's meticulous research into the history of mental health care for black Americans confirmed much of what I already knew and illuminated subjects new to me.

Some see writing as the most solitary pursuit. But anyone who writes knows the importance of having a large support team. I have been blessed in this regard. The sin of omission would be a certainty if I tried to list all of those whose help enabled me to complete this book. Even so, it would be a greater sin not to give explicit thanks to some of those very special people. My dear friend and fellow writer Debra Sampson gave me advice whenever I asked for it, and she gave encouragement whenever I needed it. George Greiff, my mentor and father figure, is no longer with us. But he contributed mightily to this book, because without him I would not be a writer. Thanking my mother, Myrtle Head, for her support during the writing of this book seems an inadequate gesture given the remarkable things she has done for me throughout my life. I must make the gesture anyway. The same can be said of the way my brothers, James, Fred, and Julius, and my sister, Patricia, have helped me toward my dreams.

I appreciate the generous terms under which Warner Bros. Publications U.S. Inc. and Bug Music granted permission to use the excerpts of blues lyrics that appear on this book's chapter title pages. No doubt, musical expression of our emotions is older than African culture. The birth of the blues provided a soundtrack for the psyches of black Americans. I recommend the Blues Heaven Foundation, founded by Willie Dixon in 1981, as a source of information on blues music. The foundation can be contacted at 2120 South Michigan Avenue, Chicago, IL 60616; by telephone at (312) 808-1286; or on the web at www.bluesheaven.com.

Finally, I offer my most heartfelt thanks to my family—to my sons Joakim, Gabriel, and Steven, and to my wife, Claire—for hanging in with me through tough times, especially during the worst of my depression. My love for the boys motivated me to finally get treatment. During the times when my struggles with depression created a vacuum in my sons' lives, Claire filled the void. She held us all together, and holds us together still.

▓ ABOUT THE AUTHOR ▓

John Head began *Black Men and Depression* as a fellow at the Carter Center Mental Health Program, where he met Kay Redfield Jamison and she agreed to write a foreword for the book. John is a former mental health reporter and features writer for the *Atlanta Journal-Constitution*. His first book, *We Were the Land's: Biography of a Homeplace,* was selected by the Georgia Writers Association as the best memoir of 1999. John has been a reporter for *USA Today* and the *Detroit Free Press* and was press secretary to Maynard Jackson when Jackson was the mayor of Atlanta. John is also the recipient of a Rosalynn Carter Mental Health Journalism Fellowship and of awards from the National Mental Health Association of Georgia and the Georgia Psychiatric Association.

Printed in the United States
by Baker & Taylor Publisher Services